To my beautiful daughter Vianlix, for making this book possible.

So many of you have asked me for this book. For years, Virginia, my personal assistant, that so many of you have met on my visitations, has asked me, «Vivian why don't you make a book with the testimonies?» I always thought it was an amazing idea, but time keeps moving on, and so years have passed.

Today, however, you hold in your hands the book that so many of you have asked me for. My journey is my Healing Ministry that has helped me walk down some really hard paths in my life, such as when I lost my oldest daughter to breast cancer. But this ministry has helped me carry that cross that is so heavy in my heart. I walk with Our Lady Guadalupe by my side always, and all the Glory goes to her son, Jesus.

As I was picking the testimonies that have gone into this book, I was astonished of the amount of love Jesus has for all of us. How he responds to the intercession of his Blessed Mother. Looking through 13 years of my Healing Ministry it was hard to only pick a few of them compared to all the ones I have received from so many of you. I can see another book in the future because for me, personally, they are all worth mentioning.

In the meantime, I will remain obedient to her

calling, to my Healing Ministry, and going to many churches doing Visitations with the Image of Our Lady of Guadalupe.

I will continue doing this journey with her until I am in her presence.

May Our Lady Guadalupe wrap you with her Holy Mantle and keep you close to her son.

Believe.

# INTRODUCTION

Vivian Mestey was born on November 10, 1954, in Manhattan, New York to Mauricio & Maria Teresa. Vivian met Felix Mestey in Puerto Rico and fell in love. They were married in 1974 and are currently enjoying 50 years of marriage. They have two daughters, Vivian C. and Vianlix.

Vivian's life took a drastic turn when her oldest daughter, Vivian C., was diagnosed with breast cancer in 2005. Two years later, her husband, Felix, was diagnosed with lymphoma. Unfortunately, Vivian herself was diagnosed in 2008 with breast cancer. She and Vivian C. received chemotherapy treatments together. Vivian's faith became much stronger because of her walk through this difficult time. She underwent two surgeries, chemotherapy, and radiotherapy. Today she is a lymphedema patient.

Through all her suffering she has surrendered to God's will. Tragically, Vivian C. lost her battle with breast cancer in 2011. After such a loss, Vivian would never have imagined that God was calling her for a special mission. But realizing that this was a call from God, Vivian accepted it obediently.

This call was to follow Our Lady of Guadalupe, and Vivian has now been the Guardian of The Image of Our Lady of Guadalupe since 2010.  Vivian travels with the image throughout the United States having visitations in Catholic Churches and Basilicas. Through this Healing Ministry, Vivian has prayed over thousands of people who have received blessings and healings through the Intercession of Our Blessed Mother, Our Lady of Guadalupe.

Holy Prayer cloths accompany this Healing Ministry. The Hail Mary is constantly prayed the entire time that these cloths are made. Prayers continue while the cloths are then being touched to the Image of Our Lady of Guadalupe. Many Miracles have transpired through the Intercession of Our Blessed Mother through the use of these cloths.

*I want to share with you some of the testimonies many of you have shared with me. Out of respect for the integrity of their testimony they have not been professionally edited and are printed in original form. In Faith there is no need for perfectionism when it comes to anyone sharing with me their faith and how Our Lady of Guadalupe has touched their lives. I hope reading them bring you closer to Her and her Beloved son Jesus! May Our Blessed Mother wrap you all with her Holy Mantal.*

# TESTIMONY

My name is Javier Montalvo, 17 years old, and I am a living example that God is good and present in our everyday lives. On January 28, 2017, I was diagnosed with a Kidney condition called Minimal Changes Disease. It was terrible to hear and process at my age. I was a strong Believer in Christ but as my condition worsened so did my faith. It became so bad at a moment I believed God sent us here to suffer and hated him for that. Yet my family members and aunt (Vivian Mestey) told me to have a little leap of faith.

I did so and wonders happened. My condition began to get itself under control and was able to live my normal life again. Also prayed and hold on to the Holy Prayer Cloth and ask Our Lady of Guadalupe for her intersession.

Now today July 26, 2017, I started my very first job. And I have to give thanks to my doctors, family but most important God.

My message for everyone today is that, when you think all hope is gone just have a little bit of faith, even if it's the size of a mustard seed. And you'll see the wonders will come to you. God has better things for you in the future, you just need to have a little bit of faith.

# TESTIMONY

---

*February 22, 2023 - Name Withheld*

My Dear Husband went into the hospital with Covid in November 2021. He was diagnosed with Afibribulation and he wasn't able to hold any food or drink down. After being in the hospital for over a week he had a catscan that showed his colon burst and he was septic. He had an emergency colon surgery with a colostomy. He remained in the hospital for 3 months with infections. His gall bladder became gangrene. He had to have it removed. My Dear Husband sometimes had 8 ivs at one time. He was very ill, and if something could go wrong it seemed to. He finally came home in late January 2022. He needed assistance with walking, standing etc. After several weeks of rehab he began to get stronger. Vivian came to our Parish in the spring of 2022 and prayed over my husband. We touched the prayer cloth to the Image of Our Lady of Guadalupe. That prayer cloth stayed with him night and day. He had another surgery in July to reverse the colostomy. He again had complications. I have more. I am saying too much.. it's only half! He had another surgery with major complications and had to refrain from food for 6 months. He developed sepsis again from the therapeutic nutrition iv. He was also receiving heavy iv antibiotics for 6 months. It was very scary and he was fragile throughout the year and dome months. We started praying the Rosary on Mondays with Vivian. After another surgery in December he started making progress. He is eating and getting stronger. He is laughing, doing chores around the house, and cooking again. He is attending Mass on weekends. He is a Miracle Man! Our Lady of Guadalupe used Ms. Vivian to bring healing physically, spiritually, and emotionally. He continues to keep the cloth on him. We have another major surgery in the near future and we are confident Our Lady of Guadalupe will bless and protect him. We are so grateful !

# TESTIMONY

*Name Withheld*

Hi Vivian!
My testimony follows by dates.

*June 7*

I met Vivian when she brought Our Lady of Guadalupe to my church, St. John the Evangelist in Warrenton. She prayed over me and I was asking for healing of my son's digestive problems. He had been suffering for 11 years. He has had many tests and doctors could not find cause. He lives over an hour away from me.

*June 8-13*

Each day I put the healing cloth over my belly while praying the Rosary of our Lady of Guadalupe. My son is Christian but not Catholic and I did not tell him I was doing this. I prayed for healing of digestive issues.

*June 14*

I learned of my 9 month-old granddaughter's ( my son's daughter)spasms that she was having and had been having for a week.

*June 15*

I was caring for my granddaughter and saw the spasms. I prayed for her, touching the cloth to her head.

*June 16*

My daughter-in-law took my granddaughter to a neurologist. The neurologist was not helpful.

*June 17*

My son and daughter-in-law tried to find a pediatric neurologist that they could see soon.

*June 18*

Vivian texted me at 8:30 pm inviting me to the Monday zoom prayer meeting. I texted her back, asking her to pray for my granddaughter. She asked for a photo of her and told me she would present the photo to Our Lady.

A little while later, Vivian said that she had fini-shed praying and that my granddaughter would be fine. I didn't know that at nearly the same time, my son and daughter-in-law had taken my grand-daughter to Children's Hospital emergency room in DC because they had been urged to go and that this was the best place.

*June 19*

12 a.m. My son texted me and said my grand-daughter's EEG would begin at 4:00 a.m. and last at least 24 hours.

*June 20*

My son texted that my granddaughter's EEG lasted 30 hours and she had NOT spasmed at all during the test. He said that the doctors said it is not 100% conclusive but it was VERY Good news!

I started praying for my son's healing again as I had been before June 14.

*June 21*

I received a text from my son. He said " I met with my dietician yesterday. She thinks my hypothesis that I cannot digest fructose properly is correct. It is a difficult thing to manage because it is very hard to identify what foods have fructose and what don't, but I have been eating whole foods that I am mostly certain. Have low fructose levels since Thursday and my stomach has been good for 5 straight days which is unprecedented in my adult memory." Vivian, I am convinced Our Lady if Guadalupe led my son to his hypothesis and that she is responsible for the healing of my granddaughter's spasms.

Praise Jesus and Mary!!!
May God bless you always!!


I believe.

# TESTIMONY

*Name Withheld*

Holy Glitter,

I went yesterday Monday to foot specialist where he put me in a ankle Brace all the way to my knee for a damage ankle. This cost me hold my husband's arm. To my shocking surprised I saw his elbow to half down his armed that he had a very deep thick layer of dry skin shell. I was so upset. He who does not allowed any kind of medications and / or care. I then attended Vivian's Monday night Rosary prayer on ZOOM. Because, my hands were full of Glitter I was trying to fine away that I may pass by my husband and touch and rubber my hands as to transmit the Graces together with the Blessed Glitters. I couldn't touch his elbow but his hair some what. I went to sleep worried and thinking of ways to care for his arm. Today he came to me and asked if I desired anything from the store. While he put his arm on the door, while talking to me I immediately notice his entire arm was healed completely.

I asked him what happened if he had cared for it even though I knew he hadn't. He said it felt like a huge rash and it hurt. But, now I am fine. So he says, please tell me what you

need from the store.. When he left the house I looked at my hands and to my amazing surprise my hands were still with Glitters.. From Monday night to today, I have washed in the morning right after waking up, washing dishes and putting hand creams, the Glitters are still on my hands, even now as I am writing this testimony as they are still on my hands. Thank you Vivian for your Divine Interceding and Blessed Ministry of Our Lady of Guadalupe

# TESTIMONY

*Name Withheld*

Month's ago I had a heart attack and recovered miraculous. For the last two days Our Lady Guadalupe has given me the manifestation of the Holy Escarchas. I was at my kitchen when my left hand got oily and full of Oil and Escarchas. And today I was at my car, the sun hit my hand, and again the manifestation of the Oil and Escarchas. Since I met Vivian Mestey years ago and also assist the Zoom rosary my life keeps changing with so many blessings. I see Our Lady of Guadalupe changing my life I.

Amen

# TESTIMONY

*Name Withheld*

I joined Vivian Mestey Monday rosary prayer group. Neither her or I never met before. As, I join the rosary on Zoom and we started to do the rosary I was in severe back pain and very worried of my ankles. Vivian at the end asked me how was my feet and legs. Now, my legs and back are pain free and the full of glitter.

Blessings.

# Testimony

Holy Prayer Cloth, Monterrey N.L. Mexico

My name is Leticia Cazares Flores, I live in Monterrey, N.L. Mexico, in the year 2020 the month of July several events occurred in my life that led me to stress and great concern derived from that I had a cerebral infarction which lasted seconds but that caused me painful consequences, I felt very bad I was with treatments, exams, medications and specialists to get me ahead of the problem but I could not feel better attached to that I had anxiety also attending to me with psychiatrist and psychologist I was very sad, I did not sleep, I cried at night because I felt that I died and having no rest that affected me a lot I felt anguish and easily lost my tranquility even having all the love and support of my family.

One day my youngest daughter came to see me with great news, a friend who had just learned what happened to me sent me a little sheet with the image of the Virgin of Guadalupe to have her by my side and so it was, when I received her I felt such great joy, I knew in my heart that she came to help me, to take care of me remember that I was not alone that I loved myself and knew what I was going through, every day I had it on my chest, I prayed the rosary with her, I thanked her for having arrived when I needed her most I felt more loved than ever, little by little I was recovering, on the other hand the doctors do not know to date what caused me the heart attack because thank God and to the intercession of our Mother has not left any sequelae in my body that usually happens in these cases and in me it was the brain, limbs and heart in which I had had greater discomfort and that indicated they could be those affected by the infarction, they were surprised that it had not reached more or had been repeated.

I, the only thing I know, is that it was a miracle of God through the intercession of the Virgin Mary who with her words full of love «Do not trouble your heart I am here that I am your Mother» filled me with comfort, strength and confidence making my faith grow more.

Today I am still in treatment with less and less medication and with great joy, taking more care of my body and more aware of how I should lead my life.

I give my testimony with great gratitude to God and to our Mother who for a long time became present in my life and has led me to know her son Jesus who has had mercy on me since there were many things that were not right in me and that I myself was provoking, with this experience I know that for something God allowed it for me well now I work to overcome them and go correcting with the help of our Mother who takes us by her hand to teach us the way to our Lord Jesus Christ. God bless you.

# TESTIMONY

*April 14, 2022 - Miracle - Emese*

Dear Vivian,

I would like to share with you the good news about my father-in-law Steve, who is 87 years old now and has been battling liver cancer for over a year and has been in and out of chemotherapy treatments.

They attended the zoom meeting with us last Monday. Along with the children we all asked for his healing.

This morning we got the news that his numbers were so good that he could drop his medication and only go in for check ups every six months !!!

Praise Our great and merciful Lord!

Praise Our Lady of Guadalupe for Her intercession yet again! For healing grandpa a second time during his fight with cancer.

You probably remember about five years ago or so he was granted his first healing from prostate cancer also by our Lady of Guadalupe when you anointed him with the Holy Oil and prayed over him during the veneration at our Parish.

We are not deserving at all, but oh so thankful for this tremendous gift from Heaven and your Healing Ministry. This Easter will be a beautiful celebration for the family, filled with thanksgiving for Our Loving Lord. Because He is GOOD ALL THE TIME!!!!

Believe in Deed!!!

# TESTIMONY

*April 1, 2022 - Miracle - Name Withheld*

Miracle through the Holy Prayer Cloth.

Diagnosis with Covid, three months in coma and pregnant. Her cousin went on, took the Holy Prayer Cloth and placed on her belly. The baby started to move and kicked. Two days later, mom had two heart attacks before the third heart attack. The baby was delivered on it own. Dr's, whereas not alert to it, physicians were treating mom on the heart issues. Not noticed, the tiny 1 pound 7 ounces baby girl was born. Today, mom and baby are home; the baby needs some therapy. After the long journey, they saw and felt the presence of Our Lady and the Mercy of Jesus.

This Miracle has changed their lives for the Glory of God.

# TESTIMONY

*January 2018 - Severe Depression*

My name is Slyvia Diaz from Puerto Rico. I'm going to tell you about my testimony. I had a severe headache y it would not go away. Le did every single text and they would not found anything on me.

One day Mrs. Vivian call me to talk ask me how was I doing? I told her and she invited me to Connecticut, that's

the church where she was going to be. I walked to the Virginy and she prayed over me and said to me « You don't have nothing, and you are Healed».

I was at the mass and then I when up to the Image of Guadalupe and touched it. I left the church I can hardly walk or talk. I was going through a severe depression, days when by and I started to feel better. The headache started to get better because the medication where not working. I thank that I when and touch the Image of Blessed Mother. It was a Miracle that I got well from that depression.

For those people that don't Believe, they should because our Virgin of Guadalupe did the Miracle and got me out of the hell that I was living. As now I doing really good and very happy.

# TESTIMONY

*Name Withheld*

Oct 8, 2020, had surgery to « repair» left larynx paralyzed during cancer surgery in 2013. Severe pain in legs after waking from anesthesia. Asked before what type would be used and I was ok with that. Was not told a muscle paralytic would also be given.

Since that date I have walked very gingerly - feeling no or very little control of leg movement. Not always using cane - being stubborn but always extremely alert to imbalance. Would use cane in equal amount of time. Tiring.

Two beautiful ladies from my Catholic Church invited me to come to Mass at St Bridget. They told me it was healing Mass but I didn't really hear that. Just wanted to go see St Bridget's again... it's so beautiful.

Was so sick the day of Healing Mass but went. Parked in handicap space and wit cane wobbled to entrance door held open by wonderful young boy.

May God reward him!

Sat in back near Jesus window. Still nagging thoughts of leaving due to increase sick feeling.

Then lines formed. I tried to stand but was having difficulty. Sweet woman behind me said to go sit in front and she would put me ahead of her when time came.

My time came. I approached the beautiful Our Lady's picture. My hand was placed on her heart, then I heard words from our hostess Vivian telling me something about Holy Spirit. But was mentally fading from her voice. Apparently I was helped to the floor.

I do remember vividly the freshness and supreme calm/relaxing aura over me and feeling - never leave!

But I «woke», moved my legs to get up, stood and felt like dancing. No pain, no wobble, just pounding heart full of joy and gratitude to Our Blessed Lord and His beautiful generous Mother. Healed!!

Praise Our Lord for His Love and Mercies. I am full of gratitude to my lady friends and to St Bridget's, AND all those involved in this healing ministry of our beautiful Lady of Guadalupe!

My heart is full of thanks forever.

# TESTIMONY

*Scott Schneider*

In February I went to my primary care provider for an annual physical. One thing I had concerns about was a constant fatigue. No matter what I did, I was exhausted and had no energy to do much of anything. My blood work came back abnormal for my liver enzymes. Three more liver enzyme checks followed that with similar numbers. At that time, I started seeking more information and appointments from specialists for the kidney, the liver and the thyroid. The thyroid doctor advised me that I had something called hyper parathyroids, and that is what was causing my fatigue. Over the course of a few months, I had multiple scans to check my parathyroid glands and I also had a bone density scan. The doctor's conclusion after the scans was still looking at the parathyroid glands. I met with a surgeon that would be conducting the surgery to remove a bad parathyroid gland. He wanted to run another test just to see if he could find out which gland was bad. The night before this scan I had Vivian pray over me as I lay there with a holy prayer cloth around my neck and throat area. The next day I went for this final scan. Praying that everything would turn out right. About a week had passed and I had a call with this surgeon. He advised me that they could not find any bad parathyroid glands and advise me that surgery would not be required. After Vivian prayed over me and holding the holy prayer cloth to my throat and neck, I have felt a decrease in my fatigue and an increased energy to do the things I used to be able to do. I always thought that Vivian's healing did not work on her family members, but I guess I was wrong, and I believe that her and our blessed mother has healed me.

# TESTIMONY

*Esme Feher*

After 40 days of ICU because of COVID, and Dr's telling family member to start do preparation for the funeral. On George pillow and always beside him and his family the Holy Prayer Cloth of Our Lady of Guadalupe. At the Event of Saturday

June 24, 2023, George in a wheel chair and with his oxygen tank was taken to the Imagen of Our Lady of Guadalupe at the Event of the Year. I was so touched to see the love on George face towards Our Lady of Guadulupe. Tears were rolling down his face and such an emotional moment for him and his family. Tears of Joy to have him there and all prayers answered. I walked each step of f this path with them, prayers, and more prayers. Our Lady of Guadalupe once again interceded with her son Jesus. Praise God, all the Glory is for him.

May Our Lady of Guadalupe wrap each one of the family with her Holy Mantle.

# TESTIMONY

*Name Withheld*

Here is testimony for my brother-in-law. I went for a visit to him and his wife. We chatted and talked about how things were going. Priests and Deacons were coming weekly and bringing Holy Communion. He was receiving chemo every week for days. I told him I brought the Our Lady of Guadalupe cloth and asked if I could put it on him and pray some prayers to Her. He said. Sure. So I prayed from my prayers in the Our Lady of Guadalupe pamphlet. Then I told him. You will be okay. 2 weeks later I was at Adoration on my lunch. My sister-in-law came unto the church and came over to me and said. WE BELIEVE CANCER IS GONE. Pet Scan showed no cancer. Amen Amen

# TESTIMONY

My 27-year-old son, was diagnosed with schizo-phrenia/bipolar

One year after graduating from high school. Understanding metal illness has only strengthened my faith and hope for some positive outcome in my son's life. I feel profound comfort in thinking about how Mary felt about her son during all of his trying times and how they impacted her. I pray for strength and her resilience that she undoubtedly had as she saw her son suffer. I have witnessed small miracles already that just fill my heart. For example, he who did not go to church school (my fail as I was raised Catholic) just last week mentioned out of the blue the Lord's Prayer and asked me what the ending was.

«For thine is the kingdom, the power and the glory, for ever and ever, Amen»

He excitedly said that was it. We then said the Our Father together a few times.

This was out of the blue while I was cleaning his laundry room after moving him into a new place. I cannot tell you how beautiful that moment was, how much happiness it gave me, and how much hope and strength.

I sleep with the our Lady of Guadeloupe cloth every night and pray for us All.

I would appreciate your prayers and any words/advice you may have to share with me.

Thank you so much for your time and positivity you provide to so many.


Only Love,
Roses and Miracle

# TESTIMONY

*Name Withheld*

Dear Vivian,

My very good friend is Raquel. About two years ago she shared your story with me and gave me my first our Lady of Guadalupe cloth. Since then I've shared your story and ministry with others. I live in a tight coastal community where most locals know each other or of each other. A friend of a friends daughter was diagnosed with cancer last year and I gifted her a cloth as I learned she was Catholic and thought she would appreciate it and understand it. A year later (just a few weeks ago) I met the mother (Victoria Bodson) in person and she shared the most beautiful story with me. She explained that her daughter had the cloth draped over her head during a very serious surgery/recovery in ICU last summer. She explained that the sterile room only had caregivers including herself covered in PPE care (no fragrances). She distinctly remembers smelling roses and not understanding why and from where it was coming from. Her daughter Gwendolyn (senior in high school sick with cancer) smelled it too. Aside from this anomaly, she said they both felt a profound sense of peace and love. She's your knows our Lady was involved. she said she will never forget that experience.

# TESTIMONY

◄•••►

*Devotion to Our Lady of Guadalupe December 8 - Name Withheld*

Candles (Velitas Colombian tradition)

There is no distances for Our Lady of Guadalupe Holy Prayer Cloth.

These little one follow grandma's devotion to Our Lady of Guadalupe. Just like grandma they walk all day with the Holy Prayer Cloth over there shoulder's.

Children live by example, grandma are a blessing in each child lives.

# TESTIMONY

*Name Withheld*

Just wanted to let you know how grateful I am to you for introducing me to that prayer cloth from Our Lady of Guadalupe.

Had knee replacement surgery in early August and have been putting the cloth on my repaired knee every night with good results. Have been fortunate to have had minimal pain/swelling throughout the recovery process and am now (2 weeks later) able to walk more, do some gardening and even drive a little.

Power of prayer!
God is good!

Take care, many thanks,

# TESTIMONY

*Name Withheld*

Hi Vivian miracles on unborn baby!

A fellow, parishioner, and his wife share with me that their daughter, 18 weeks pregnant with her first child, has just been told that preliminary test indicate her baby had problems, probably Spina Bifida. A sonogram was scheduled to be performed at 20 weeks at which time a more precise diagnose could be made, according to her doctors. The family was understandably, worried and distraught. Another Parishioner and I said we would pray for them and their daughter and grandchild. I had recently purchased a prayer cloth of Our Lady of Guadalupe, which I offered to this couple to use for praying with her daughter- they gratefully excepted. About three weeks later, I got an email from this people stating that their daughters doctor report that the baby now appears normal and healthy and everything looks good! They share that they and their daughter strongly believe it was an interception of Our Lady that healed this unborn child. God be praised for his wonderful mercy!!!

# TESTIMONY

*Name Withheld*

I believe God puts dreams in our hearts. They were meant to lead us through our purpose -are journey here on earth. Four as long as I can re- member, my dream was to be a mother. I always wanted a large family, and to stay home and raise my babies.

My husband and I married 4 1/2 years ago in 2010, and shortly after I was heartbroken to hear a doctor say I will probably never have children due a medical complication. I refuse to accept that as truth for me. Again, I believe God put that dream in my heart, and I refuse to believe he could put that desire there, and then not allow it to happen! We try for years with no sign that our prayers are being answered, but I stood on this promise from Jesus:

(Mark 11:22-25) "have faith in God," Jesus answer. "truly I tell you, if anyone says to this moun- tain, ' go, throw yourself into the sea,' and does not doubt in the heart but believes that what they say will happen, it will be done for them. Therefore, I tell you, whatever you asked for in prayer, believe that you have received it, and it will be yours. And when you stand, praying, if you hold anything against anyone, forgive them, so that your Father in heaven, may forgive you your sins."

In January 2014, my mom told me about the image of our lady of Guadalupe. She said that the image would be at Holy Trinity and that we should go. My husband and I both went to see the image. We went together, and when we touch Our Lady, her hands and belly were warm. Vivian and Robert then press the image against my abdomen and pray over me.

On March 1, 2014 I have had this overwhelming feeling to take a pregnancy test. I was taking medications for migraines, and I remember thinking that if I was pregnant, I would need to stop those medications. I was not having any pregnancy symptoms, I just had a feeling. When the test came back positive, my husband and I were filled with unimaginable joy!

I believe that a miracle came to us through our lady of Guadalupe. We went to see the image in January, and the next month I conceived! Ninth month later on November 4th, I gave birth to our beautiful, perfect Noah Patrick. In all my life I have never known a love such as this. He is the sweetest most beautiful gift from God. God is so good! And to this day, mama Mary is showering Noah with her presence. We find holy glitter left on his head all the time! I take comfort, knowing she has him in her protection. I am now blessed to be a stay at home mother on this journey, striving to be a holy family....

Have faith! Believe!

# TESTIMONY

*Mary S.*

My name is Mary S. In January 2013, I return to the Catholic Church due to a series of miraculous event. A few months later, I went to the fertility specialist to figure out why my husband and I had not conceived a baby after actively trying for two years. I learned that I had a host of fertility issues which were lightly preventing a pregnancy. I understood from my faith that I could not accept IVF or artificial insemination, which the specialist had strongly recommend, so I started praying. In September, at the advice of my spiritual director, Father Andrews, my husband and I pray a special prayer. Read aloud the gospel of Saint Luke's account of Saint Elizabeth miraculous pregnancy. We also pray palms 23 together with Father Andrews. The same week, our parish was blessed to host the image of Our Lady of Guadalupe. When I shared my infertility problems with the guardian of our Lady's image, Vivian Mestey, she kindly allow me to press my belly to our Lady's Image. Vivian also said a special prayer for me. I remember feeling a sense of love when I glazed upon Our Lady Image. Two weeks later, I discovered I was pregnant. The timing of that pregnancy coincides with Our Lady's

Visit to our parish (as well as the prayers, my husband and I did along sign our spiritual director, Father Andrews.) I have no doubt that Our Lady intercede on behalf of our little family. Now I am the blessed mother of a sweet and beautiful little girl. Thank you to Vivian and to all those involved in guarding over and sharing Our Lady of Guadalupe's image.

# TESTIMONY

*A miraculous testimony from a liver transplant*

In January 2014, my husband was diagnosed with liver cancer. According to the doctors, the cancer could spread if they try to remove it, so they decided to do a Tase procedure, which could be stabilize the cancer, in hopes that it would not spread. He was then put on a liver transplant list in April at Georgetown Hospital in Washington DC & at the university of Mary Washington in Baltimore. Both my husband and I have a lot of faith in the virgin of Guadalupe as did both of our parents before us. I call a very good friend of ours, Vivian Mestey, who had The digital image of our lady of Guadalupe at her home. Vivian 's family & a few of our friends pray over my husband. My husband approached the picture of Our Lady & placed the fingertips of his left hand on her mantle & his right hand over her hands. While he was praying, he experienced a tremendous amount of heat on his left hand &

had to pull his hand away from the picture. While he was praying, Vivian placed her hand over his liver and the area got so hot that he had to move her hands away. Some of the ladies there experienced tingling fingers. It was all a beautiful experience! The week after the prayerful experience, my husband & I were at daily Mass & had just come back from receiving Holy Communion. While we were kneeling down, giving prayerful things, my husband felt a hand reach across his side, & on top of his liver. When he open his eye, he looked down to see if anyone was touching him. No one was around. He asked me if I had to try to get his attention, but I did not. He felt that somehow this was Divine Intervention!

In late May & early June, he was called as he translate recipient backup twice & on the third time, he was told that they had a good match for him at Georgetown hospital even though he was told he was the third back up. We have prayed for Georgetown hospital since it was a Catholic hospital & we were impressed with the staff that we had met. Everything was so miraculous! We were met at the hospital by our two daughters, our son and his wife. The surgeons we were hoping for, wasn't due to be on that evening, but he was asked to cover for the surgeon who was out of town. The surgery was to take 6 to 12 hours, but only took 4 1/2. The average unit of blood received for a liver transplant is 4 units of blood. He only receive 1 unit of blood, that ICU nurse said that his post operation results were a joke, and that no one gets those numbers right after surgery. His recovery has been amazing! He has felt no pain associated with the surgery only a feeling of tightness across his stomach area. He was sitting down after two days, walking & climbing stairs. He always looked great and still does! He was told that he would be in the hospital for at least 4 1/2 weeks, but was discharged after 8 days. The staff was amazed by his progress! One of the nurses said he didn't want him to leave as he spoke with her and most patients did not because they couldn't. It has been a little over a month now & he is eating very well, walking on the treadmill, driving, and back to most normal activity. He took a cloth with the image of our lady of Guadalupe on it to the hospital & how had it on his pillow, next to him. He received many comments about our lady and a doctor even commented that "she is very powerful!"

We certainly can attest to that!

The Holy Glitter (Escarchas) abounds around

her. She miraculously shed tears and Holy Oil is sometimes filled on her hair and mental. Her eyes open and closed. Some hear her heartbeat & also Jesus heartbeat.

She is truly miraculous! Through her intersection, many are healed! Thank you for this wonderful ministry of the traveling image of Our Lady of Guadalupe which travel around the United States. She is truly needed in these times!

# Testimony

*Breast cancer testimony - Alba R Hincapie*

My name is Alba, I was diagnostic with breast cancer; my mammogram showed two tumors in my right breast, I was devastated. I had to stop further test, because I had to travel to my country and take care of my mother that is very sick. My good friend Shakyra told me to call her aunt Mrs. Vivian Mestey, who is the guardian of our Lady of Guadalupe. A very faithful lady. I did call Vivian, I spoke with her. She prayed over the phone with me and she also prayed in tongues. While praying, I felt a sensation of tingling in my breast, and also felt chills. At the same time, I felt like warm water running through my breast. I was overwhelmed of what I was feeling. Mrs. Mestey told me, "Go on your trip to Columbia, and when you come back for the biopsy, they won't have to do it. Because they are not going to find anything and you will be healed." Every single day since that conversation on September 23, 2015, it kept playing in my mind;

those words will give me the comfort for the weeks to come. While I was on the plane to travel to Colombia, I got a sharp pain in my breast. And as always, I will hear Vivian 's words. I got my prayer cloth and also took some home. I told my dad. "Please put it over mom that is very ill." I told him, "this very faithful lady told me to use it". He replied " Let me know what your results are." I answered, "I will". I slept every day with my prayer cloth, and Vivian 's words kept giving me the support that I needed to overcome the fear that I was feeling.

I came back home in the month of December 2015 and was scheduled to get the biopsy for the surgery. While in the procedure, the doctor was trying to locate the tumors. The doctor couldn't find it. He was very surprise, and therefore I was scheduled to get an MRI. Again, Praise God, and Our Lady of Guadalupe, nothing couldn't be located. Amen! The doctors where unable to find anything. Yes!!!! I am cancer free. I am so blessed that our lady of Guadalupe interceded with my healing. I am also blessed to have the prayer cloth and the blessings that I have a second chance. I pray every day for Mrs. Vivian Mestey, that God, and our lady of Guadalupe, protect her and give her the blessings of helping others, as she helped me.

# TESTIMONY

*EF*

I was in Washington DC on October 1, 2011, at the Shrine of the Immaculate Conception and got to see our Lady of Guadalupe briefly as the team in charge was getting ready to take her to the next destination. My sister has encouraged me to ask our Lady for anything. For about five years, we have been praying to have the blessing of a baby. Medically my chances are a lot smaller to conceive, then of an average healthy woman of my age. Our only options were and are to this day prayers and adoption. Our prayers were answered above and beyond. I was blessed with an easy, most beautiful pregnancy without any complications, a beautiful and easy birth (less than 2 hours) and a healthy beautiful baby girl name Mary born in June 2012. I have returned to see the relic of our lady again while I was about 5-6 months pregnant and have taken my daughter back as well after she was born. I discover something new about her every time I visit. Thank you mother

Mary for you are so GOOD, LOVING and your blessings are so plentiful! I love you, Jesus!

# TESTIMONY

*MC*

Saint Timothy Church/ Chantilly

It was 2014 when the image came around St Timothy's church. Surely before that, I was diagnosed with thyroid cancer.

I decided to visit the image and pray that the Lady of Guadalupe will help me through this ordeal. I stood in line. I told the lady in charge of the image (I believe Miss Vivian Mestey) how scared I am, and was hoping the cancer did not really spread.

SHE LOOKED AT ME STRAIGHT IN MY EYES, AND SAID WITH CERTAINTY- NO, IT DID NOT!

Wow, I was amazed, still, I doubted. Then it was my turn in front of the image. I was trying to pray when a lady kept telling me look, look, there is glitter. Due to my bad hearing, I did not understand the glitter part, that was explained beforehand. She said the glitter came as I kneeled in front of the image. Really I said....Wow.... What does it mean? She explain.

I was told to take a tape and get some glitter. Fine, I was thinking, why not.

I try so hard to get some glitter, saw it, but wouldn't stick to the tape. I surely was disappointed? I only got one whites speck on my tape. I left.

On the way driving home. It hit me. White? Yes! It is my sign/answer from Mary-white-meaning "clean" " no cancer".... My glitter!

Sure enough, my operation went well and not only did the NOT spread, it was small, I did not even need the radio, active pill or chemo or anything unpleasant.

I may not have heard Mary's heartbeat or felt her warm hands, but I know Mary was communicating with me in her way, and to Miss Vivian too. For I sure would have been back this year to tell her " you are wrong" -but she was right

# TESTIMONY

*April 1, 2020 - Miracles  - Name Withheld*

Miracle through the holy prayer cloth.

Dino's with Kovic, three months in coma and pregnant. Her cousin went on, took the Holy Prayer Cloth and place it on her belly. The baby started to move and kicked two days later, mom had two heart attacks before the third heart attack. The baby wants the liver on it own. Doctors, whereas not alert to it. Physicians were treating mom on the heart issue. Not noticing, the tiny, 1 lbs. seven oz baby girl was born today, mom and baby are home; the baby needs some therapy. After the long journey, they saw, and felt the presence of Our Lady and the Mercy of Jesus.

This miracle has changed your lives for the Glory of God .

# TESTIMONY,

## PHYSICAL HEALING

*March 10, 2016 - Dyhalma Nolla De Trudell*

I went to visit our Virgin De Guadalupe in Fredericksburg, Virginia. In Thanksgiving for the safe delivering of my grandson, Thomas Mateo, my family, and I arrive early. My sister, Myrna Nolla-Horner, I had given my daughter, Karlie Estrada, a blessed cloth, to place over her pregnancy belly for safe delivery. As you will see from her testimony, Thomas Mattea was delivered safely and healthy. As we were being encouraged to come forward to touch our blessed mother, I told my son Shawn, who is wheelchair-bound with Cerebral Palsy, that I would be right back, and that I needed to buy some cloths. When I came back into the church there was a line. I took my place in line and waited. Vivian turned around haven't finished helping another faithful person, when she looked around to the end of the line and saw me. She then said "are you not his mother?" Pointing to Shawn. Yes, I am. Come up here. You don't need to stand in line, I have been waiting for you. I look at Shawn and we went up front. Vivian shared the miracle and blessing being brought forth, she covered him with the Blessett cloth and told me not to remove it. Tuesday, March 15, 2016, I went to reconciliation, I have been away from this sacrament for 10 years. I am and have been welcome back. The next day, I went to my doctor for physical therapy. 4 1/2 years ago I was in a car accident that left me in constant debilitating pain affecting the whole right side of my body. I had to use an orthotic/brace to walk. When my doctor check my length, and I was pain-free and could feel my foot. I was flabbergasted, didn't know what to make/believe of it. I am healed! As each day goes by, I have no option, but to accept this wonderful blessing. I am slowly sharing my miraculous healing, I am pain-free, have total use return to my right side of the body end, and I'm joyful. Starting to shout it from the mountain tops-

# Testimony

---

*Dyhalma Nolla De Trudell - Prayers answer - Name Withheld*

Dear Miss Mestey,

We wanted to tell you about a testimony. When you were here in Virginia in Saint Timothy church with mother of Guadalupe, we pray for having a second baby.

God has granted our wish and we are due in August.

My wife always keeps the Mary's cloth on her tummy.

Please pray for us
Thank you!

# TESTIMONY

*Name Withheld*

Vivian, I would like to share my story…

We met you at the Saint Veronica in Chantilly on March 3, 2016. You prayed with me for my mama, who we were going to see right after. My friend and I saw crazy bright glitter in her room that night. We gave mom the cloth and the rosary that a little girl mysteriously handed me after I pray with you. My mom was suffering from Alzheimer's, and I pray that God prepare a place for her. She was about the same as she has been for several months, worried, and in a wheelchair, unsettle Thursday night. Friday she started to have trouble breathing and swallowing. We returned to you Friday at a different church to thank you for your prayers and share our glitter story. Friday night she stayed on oxygen, by Saturday she was sleeping peacefully in her bed. She got her eternal reward and freedom from the disease on Monday. Thursday night when we gave

her the cloth, was the last conscious visit with her. Her view from her bed was the picture below. She finally got her reward for a life Well lived…

*Saturday 7:59 AM*

Thursday I brought the Mary statue from the dresser closer to mom. She had been staring across the room at it. I do not think our visit to the Guadalupe picture and our time with you was a coincidence with mom end to suffering. Many suffer from this disease for years. Mom's health change very quickly that weekend. We miss her so much but I do feel joy for her freedom.

# TESTIMONY

*Highly allergic to peanut - John*

Hello, my name is John and I would like to talk about how I was healed by the Virgin Mary. It all started when I was in sixth grade on Christmas, I had a piece of candy with peanut butter and I became very sick, I was rushed to the hospital, and we find out I was extremely allergic to peanuts whenever exposed to peanuts. I will have anaphylaxis. I started to carry an EpiPen wherever I had to go.

I had different Test and I was diagnosed as highly allergic to peanut. My mom mentioned about the miraculous image of our lady of Guadalupe at Saint Mary Church, and we went to see her. When I touch her, I felt her heartbeat, the oil on her hair and babies Jesus in her womb. It was amazing!! I asked her to cure me from my allergies to peanuts.

Next month we went to see another specialist for allergy, and after doing some evaluation he couldn't find any kind of reaction to peanuts. The doctor said I cannot find any allergy to peanuts!! He was unexplainable because it was so severe before that I could never be around peanuts. Now I can eat peanuts and smell peanuts without getting sick anymore. The blessed virgin mother has blessed me, and it makes me feel amazed that I was helped in the hardest time of my life. It was hard for my family, and especially me, but no matter how much you are suffering God will always come to help you and he will help you in the hardest moments, in your struggles in life, he will always be there. I believe that I was tested by my faith with this allergy I always had to eat in separate rooms I had to be by myself, almost all the time, but now I can be a regular kid again, thanks to our blessed mother.

God bless, John

# TESTIMONY

*Margaret*

Vivian, my son wrote his testimony I wanted to let you know on the way to my house, the prayer cloth that we bought became really warm. To the point that they would burn our hands.

That night in my son's room, he found in his guitar a lot of glitter..........The next day I found them also on the steering wheel of my car.

Take care, and thank you for your ministry.

# Testimony

---

*Frozen shoulder - Marisin Fabrega*

My name is Marisin Fabrega in September 2015. I had scheduled surgery for my left shoulder. Which I have been in pain every single day. Time pass by and my arm lost strength and little by little. I was unable to lift it up. I went to a lot physical therapy, but nothing helped. I was referred to a specialist, he recommended surgery because I had 'frozen shoulder' and only surgery would fix the damage. I decided to wait because I was in the transition of changing job. In one occasion, I went to see Dr. orthodontic for my braces appointment. She's Catholic y told me " that in her church Saint Mary's Catholic Church was going to be expose the image of a lady of Guadalupe. I went there with lots of faith, and I got the prayer cloth. Slept with it a lot of nights, and today I can say "I Been Healed"

I don't need surgery. I Believe!

Amen…

# TESTIMONY

*Twin babies - Name Withheld*

Today, two years and six months, I visit the virgin of Guadalupe, the same as today 3-3-16. And asked that I could have my twin babies because I had complicated pregnancy. I give thanks to the virgin of Guadalupe, I had them. They're healthy, they're two years old. And thank you for the people that make it possible for this blessing. May God bless them today, tomorrow, and always. Thank your Mother for being our Mother and for interceding. The mom of twins.

# TESTIMONY

*Name Withheld*

The night before the event, my dog had choked, and I pray the Our Father and Hail Mary. After the prayers, my dog got better and I felt it was a miracle because he was fading and I couldn't do anything was going to take him to the vet, about 20 miles from home , I was sad and did the only thing that I could do, pray.

I was so thankful to God and the virgin for helping my dog get better. I had tears of joy. The next day, I went to see the digital image of the virgin of Guadalupe, it was my first time. I stood in line with my friend, and then they told us to come back after mass. We did, and had were able to experience what many had said. I was able to hear her heartbeat and felt her hands warm. I did not feel the womb, I guess I was rushing because they were others waiting

After everyone saw the painting, I went back

in the line, so I could calmly experience hearing the heartbeat of baby Jesus, but unfortunately, I couldn't. I prayed and thought that it was not the time. When I got home, I told my husband about my experience, after my dog greeted me. We had dinner and relaxed. My dog usually follows me everywhere, and when I went to pet him, I noticed a good sparkle on his nose, it was in the right side. I thought it could be a drop of water since I had wash my hands before, but I remember I dry them. It was a good sparkle. I was very happy to see it.

Later, when I was sitting in the rocking chair, I looked down the floor, left of my feet and saw a blue sparkle. I was amazed, since there was no way a blue sparkle get into the house- we haven't had a birthday celebration in a while, and I have swept the floor many times. I prayed and was happy.

Time went by, and I checked my dog, and the sparkle was gone. I also checked the floor and nothing. I feel the sparkles were there to remind me that she was with me. They disappear later, because there is no need to see, if there is faith

" Blessed are those who believe yet do not see.".

# Testimony of Pregnancy

*MF*

Thanks for the miracle of my blessed virgin of Guadalupe my daughter was born perfect. My virgin mother of Guadalupe protected me while I was pregnant and expecting my daughter. Because she protected me and watch over me, I named my daughter Guadalupe, after my blessed mother of Guadalupe.

# TESTIMONY

*HD.*

Last week, Vivian was having healing with the image of Guadalupe at my dear friends Maria's house. Due to the raining, I could not attend. They came afterwords to my house at midnight to see and pray with me. Vivian used the prayer cloth of our lady and we pray on a picture of my sick mother in rehab. Who was unable to walk.

We use a recent picture I took of her. We all three pray for one hour. Vivian also prayed over me, as I am disabled with multiple issues. Two days later, I went to see mom with the cloth Vivian gave me. I pray over mom using this same holy cloth. Three days later while mom was with physical therapy.... My brother walked in to see her on her feet, using a walker and taking steps with the therapist. I attribute this miracle to our Lady of Guadalupe, Vivian , and all the powerful prayers having been said. All happening within five days. Thank you Jesus for this miracle and for the power and grace you bestowed upon your faithful servants. Please continue to pray for mom's progress that she may return home for her 94th birthday March,15th.

God bless you Vivian.

# TESTIMONY

*Yvonne Garcia*

In October they withdraw a mass, size of a ball that I had in my left breast. Months pass by, and all of the sudden I felt pain in my left breast. When I went back to the doctor, he told me. "that it was growing". I didn't know what he was talking about. Then he started to explain. "that an ultrasound, that he did an August show that I have something under my left breast." The doctor never called to let me know I had something. He order more tests on me. My friend Rocio lent me the Prayer Cloth with the image of Our Mother of Guadalupe for three days. When I went back to get the results, the blessed mother had heal me. The doctor said " that what I had, disappear." I want to thank our Virgin for the Miracle.

# TESTIMONY

*Guardian witnesses Holy Glitter on the Missionary Image - Name Withheld*

Guardian Vivian Mestey wrote to me from South Carolina that the missionary image, manifested holy glitter, during a visitation that she hosted. She wrote, not only was oil present, but also Holy Glitter on the Missionary image of our lady of Guadalupe. It was on her hair and on her forehead near her left eye. You could see a small cross, looking from the front of the image. The Holy Glitter on her forehead was gold colored. A young boy pointed out the cross and the color. After a while, some people pointed out that they was Holy Glitter on the floor. People were getting on their knees to pick them up…. It was one blessing after another…. Our lady of Guadalupe was bringing miracles for all in need.

# TESTIMONY

*Karen Restivo*

My name is Karen Restivo. I suffered an injury to my left knee on May 20th of this year. Because of pain and swelling, I was unable to keep up with daily routine for 10 days. My doctor took x-rays and said that nothing was broken but I suffered a sprain to my ligaments. She gave me a prescription for an anti-inflammatory and pain meds and said to expect a recovery period to be 3 to 4 months and to wear a knee brace.

After hearing about Vivian Mestey ministries' devotion to our Lady of Guadalupe from family members, I reached out to Vivian to invite her to bring our Lady's image to visit Serenity Matagorda Isle in Texas. Vivian agreed to take part in healing service at our Lady of Guadalupe Catholic Church in Bay City, Texas. Two healing services were helped on June 13th & 14th. I went before our Lady's image the evening of the 13th. That night, I struggled to sleep because of the severe pain up and down my left leg. During the healing service of the 14th, Vivian laid hands and prayed over me. That night there was no pain during my sleep. The next morning there was no pain. I went to appointments throughout the day on the 15th with no necessary for a knee brace. That evening, we went down to the beach and walk together and celebrated our Lady's healing powers in the name of her son Jesus Christ. I'm so thankful for my healing.

# TESTIMONY

*Name Withheld*

When I was diagnosed with stage four advanced small cell carcinoma throughout my dominant area, I took it upon myself to stay positive, and look for ways to trust in my faith to get me through my journey. I heard our Lady of Guadalupe would be visiting at Saint Mary's Parish And decided to attend. I was very moved by the experience and after talking to Vivian she asked if she could pray for me. I then went for my PET and CAT scan a few weeks later and receive wonderful news! Everything seem to be shrinking after only three rounds of chemo therapy. I continue with chemo and once again, ask Vivian for prayers to get me through my six round of chemo check-up; this time my doctor said everything from before was gone, no new growth, nothing lit up with cancer! I believe that Vivian 's prayers, encouragement, and laying of the hands helped confirm my believe in God's Mercy and wonderful, healing powers, if we put our faith to work.

# TESTIMONY

<hr>

*June 16, 2016 - Microscopic Collagenous Colitis - Name Withheld*

In November 2010 I was diagnosed as having Microscopic Collagenous Colitis. This is a very debilitating intestinal ailment that cost constant loose bowels, bloating, and some pain. The gastroenterologist prescribe steroids, which I have to take for two weeks. As you know steroids have many side effects that are not good. I got a little bit better, but the problem did not go away and in a week after I stop taking the steroids my intestines were just as bad or perhaps worse than before. I did some research and started taking some supplements which help me some. However, the problem continues off and on. I will be OK for a couple of weeks and then would start with the same problem again. I also had to be careful with what I ate. When I heard what the image of our Lady of Guadalupe was going to be in display at Saint Timothy church in March this year, I immediately thought of going to church and see it. When I got in line, I told you what my problem was, I follow your instruction, and got closer to the image of our Lady of Guadalupe with my stomach lightly touching it. I feel like a tingling throughout my body which is hard to explain. I sat down and said a prayer and thank Our Lady for helping me get well. Before I left church, I bought a cloth that has her image. Since that day, I have had no problems at all with my intestine. I am completely normal and if I'm not mistaken, it's been almost 2 months since I saw the image of our Lady of Guadalupe at Saint Timothy Church. This is really a miracle that I will never ever forget. I have faith and I believe.

# TESTIMONY

*Brain tumor - Name Withheld*

First of all, the honor and glory is to God, who put people in our path to use them as an intercessor to make his plans perfect. I would like to share this awesome MIRACLE, his name is Joselito, from Panama City, Panama. He was diagnosed with a brain tumor call "olfactory groove meningioma" it is a common tumor that grows slowly in your brain and only presents problem when is big.

The only symptoms he presents was the loss of vision in his left eye, and migraine once in a while. As you know, just the fact that is brain it is scary, but we were never prepare for what was coming. The doctor. (neurosurgeon) talked to our family and share his concern, it was a giant tumor, 6" x 5" x 6". The surgery high risk because it was sitting in the bottom of the brain and involves many sensory areas around the brain. I remember he said: I will do my best, we only have to pray, and we did.

I contacted Vivian and ask her to pray for my

brother, and I sent her a picture of him. She immediately answer, and said: believe he is healed, his picture has been placed next to our lady of Guadalupe.

Well, my brother was waiting for surgery, the piece of cloth of our lady of Guadalupe was given to him. He used to sleep with it, and pray for healing every day. His surgery lasted nine hours, very difficult. I remember seeing the doctors face with concern. He survived the surgery!!! Now we have to wait. 48 hours had passed, and my brother went critical near death. The doctors talk to us and said: be prepare, we are losing him. It was devastating for us, but instead of getting sad, we reinforce the prayers. Two of my sisters spent hours with a piece of cloth of our Lady and lost count of how many rosaries and prayers. To the Glory of God and his Holy Mother, he survived. He spent 30 days more in the hospital, minor things happen, but he is healed. I remember one of the nurses staff said to me: where is this piece of cloth of the virgin, your brother used to put it on his face every night before the surgery.

The lady of Guadalupe once again, show her love and gave him an opportunity to live, the beauty of all is that a tumor was BENING!!! Amen!

Joselito is recovering at home, needs to rest for at least 3 months, he is normal and better than before, his mind is clear, alert, and he can see everything. He is happy and thankful, and blessed to be able to raise his 10 year old son.

Thank you, Vivian, for your prayers. My faith is stronger, and will never doubt, that if we believe and pray for miracles, it will happen. Amen.

# TESTIMONY

*JR*

Hi
Vivian,

I just wanted to let you know that all of the volunteers that helped you last week at Saint Veronica have had prayers answer, a tribute to the intersection of our lady of Guadalupe.

I don't have details on the others, but my wife receive a job offer today. She has been unemployed for eleven months. She starts work this Wednesday.

I wanted to thank you for your dedication to our lady. You have inspired me to a deeper devotion to her. I was honored to be a small part of a very special event as St Veronica.

God bless

# TESTIMONY

*May 2 - Shakyra*

Do you believe in miracles???

I do!!

It's not about what religion you are it's about faith!!

I would like to share one with you, because I'm sure there is someone out there who needs a Miracle in their life.

Last Saturday I end up in the hospital it has been two days of heavy, bleeding a big no-no after my surgery.

So I go in there, we're checking and they said "we don't see anything from the outside but if you keep bleeding, we have to take you to surgery because it can be something rip internally".

My face change in my head I was like surgery again "eso no era" no way! :(

So, my aunt called me, Titi, Vivian Mestey

She was very concerned, and was like "They said what? Surgery no, no!!"

So, all of a sudden she stopped talking and I knew she was praying. Then she said "when they come to check you in an hour there will be no more bleeding. No more pain"

Sure enough I walked out of the hospital and today— a week and a day later— no more bleeding and the pain is gone.

I share this because it's not the first time this happened when she prays over me, she has a gift of healing.

Go into Escarchas of Guadalupe read all the testimony that she gets daily from people all over that she has prayed for, even over the phone. I have seen the ones that have happened with people close to me!!

She will be in Orlando in late May if you are in need of healing, please contact me.

All it takes is faith. God will do the rest!!!!

I believe!

Everyone has a story, and she can relate with a lot of you out there.

*www.vivianmestey.com*

# Believe

## Vivian Mestey

Healing Ministry Through the Intercession of Our Lady of Guadalupe

A mi hermosa hija, Vianlix, por hacer posible
este libro.

Muchos de ustedes me pidieron este libro. Virginia, mi asistente personal, que muchos han conocido en mis visitas, llevaba años diciéndome: «Vivian, deberías escribir un libro con los testimonios». Siempre pensé que era una excelente idea, pero el tiempo vuela y los años van pasando. Sin embargo, hoy tienen en sus manos el libro que me pidieron. Mi camino es el Ministerio de Sanación, que me ha ayudado a superar momentos muy duros en mi vida, como cuando perdí a mi hija mayor a causa de un cáncer de mama. Pero este ministerio me ha ayudado a llevar esa cruz tan pesada en mi corazón. Siempre camino con Nuestra Señora Guadalupe a mi lado, y toda la gloria es para su hijo Jesús.

Mientras seleccionaba los testimonios que aparecen en este libro, me sorprendió la cantidad de amor que Jesús tiene por todos nosotros, y cómo responde a la intercesión de su santísima madre. Revisar 13 años de Ministerio de Sanación fue difícil, ya que había muchos testimonios para elegir. Puedo vislumbrar otro libro en el futuro porque, para mí, todos son valiosos y dignos de mención.

Mientras tanto, seguiré obedeciendo a su llamado, a mi Ministerio de Sanación y visitando muchas más iglesias llevando la imagen de Nuestra Señora de Guadalupe. Seguiré haciendo este viaje con ella hasta que esté en su presencia. Que Nuestra Señora de Guadalupe los cubra con su santo manto y los mantenga cerca de su hijo. Crean.

Vivian Mestey

# Introducción

Vivian Mestey nació el 10 de noviembre de 1954 en Manhattan (Nueva York), y es hija de Mauricio y María Teresa. Vivian conoció a Félix Mestey en Puerto Rico y se enamoraron. Se casaron en 1974 y llevan 50 años felizmente casados. Tienen dos hijas, Vivian C. y Vianlix.

La vida de Vivian dio un giro drástico cuando a su hija mayor, Vivian C., le diagnosticaron cáncer de mama en 2005. Dos años después, a su marido, Félix, le diagnosticaron linfoma. En 2008, a la propia Vivian le diagnosticaron cáncer de mama. Ella y su hija mayor recibieron quimioterapia juntas. La fe de Vivian se fortaleció mucho durante este difícil momento. Se sometió a dos operaciones, quimioterapia y radioterapia. Hoy es paciente de linfedema. A pesar de todo su sufrimiento, se ha entregado a la voluntad de Dios. Por desgracia, su hija mayor, Vivian C. perdió la batalla contra el cáncer de mama en 2011. Después de tal pérdida, Vivian nunca habría imaginado que Dios la estaba llamando para una misión especial. Sin embargo, al darse cuenta de que era un llamado divino, Vivian lo aceptó obediente.

Este llamado consistía en seguir a Nuestra Señora de Guadalupe, y Vivian ha sido la guardiana de la imagen de Nuestra Señora de Guadalupe desde 2010. Viaja con la imagen por los Estados Unidos, visitando iglesias católicas y basílicas. A través de este Ministerio de Sanación, Vivian ha rezado por miles de personas que han recibido bendiciones y sanaciones a través de la intercesión de nuestra santísima madre, Nuestra Señora de Guadalupe.

Los sagrados paños acompañan a este Ministerio de Sanación. Durante todo el proceso de confección de los paños, se reza constantemente la avemaría. Las oraciones continúan mientras los paños son tocados con la imagen de Nuestra Señora de Guadalupe. Muchos milagros han ocurrido a través de la intercesión de nuestra santísima madre mediante el uso de los sagrados paños.

*Quiero compartir algunos de los testimonios que muchos de ustedes me han dado. Por respeto a sus testimonios, no han sido editados profesionalmente. No hay necesidad de buscar la perfección cuando alguien comparte conmigo su fe y cómo Nuestra Señora de Guadalupe ha cambiado su vida. Espero que su lectura los acerque más a ella y a su amado hijo Jesús. Que nuestra madre bendita los envuelva a todos con su santo manto.

# TESTIMONIO

*Junio 26, 2023*

Sorda de un oído desde nacimiento
"¡Efatá!" (es decir "¡Ábrete!")
La noche del 26 de Junio de 2023 y amaneciendo el 27 cambiaron mi vida. Luego de rezar el rosario a la Virgen de Guadalupe y de una larga plática en un grupo del cual sólo quedábamos tres personas: Vivían, otra mujer y yo; expresé de manera casual que yo nací sorda por el oído derecho. Vivían elevó la mirada. Hubo pausa y silencio. Luego se levantó fue a la imagen de la Virgen de Guadalupe. Me pregunta; "cuál oído es?" Le respondí, el derecho, y mirando la imagen colocó sus manos sobre el oído derecho de la imagen de la Virgen. Me pidió que pusiera el Pañito Sagrado sobre mi oído sordo ("el malo"). Comenzó a orar intensamente pidiendo con amor "sanación, sanación, sanación".

Al cabo de un rato, silencio. Abro los ojos y la miro. Me preguntó qué sentía. Volvió a preguntar.

Yo no sabia que decir. Mientras ella oraba yo sentí un "pop" en mis huesos zigomático y occipital. La única manera que yo podría confirmar si estaba oyendo era a través de una llamada telefónica. Mi oído izquierdo (el bueno) siempre va a interferir pues está sobre desarrollado para compensar la falta de audición del otro.

Contesté la llamada emocionante que me hizo Vivian. Yo quedé perpleja. Metí el dedo en el oído izquierdo para evitar escuchar por él…. ¡Estaba oyendo el teléfono por el oído derecho por primera vez en mi vida!!!! ¡No lo podía creer! Sí, creía lo que pasaba pero era increíble esa sensación. Fueron tantas y tantas las veces que en el pasado me coloqué el teléfono en el oído derecho y nada. Los que me conocen bien lo saben.

Escuché! Escuché!!! Mi cara lo decía todo!!!! Fue igual de emotivo que los video en YouTube de niños que escuchan por primera vez. Esa fui yo la madrugada de junio 27.

La Virgen me quiere, la Virgen intercedió ante Dios. Bendita sea! Yo soy testigo y producto de lo que hace Nuestra Madre y del gran poder de la fe y amor de Dios.

Luego de secar las lágrimas, llamé a mis hijas. Ellas quedaron atónitas! Mami!!!! Recibiste un milagro!!!! Yo solo estaba feliz de escuchar sus voces por primera vez en mi oído derecho. Ahora el "oído nuevo". El oído abierto! Dios es bueno! Gracias por tu intercesión Virgen de Guadalupe!

# TESTIMONIO

*Prolapso Uterino*

LE DOY GRACIAS A DIÓS Y A LA SEÑORA VIVIAN POR SIEMPRE SER UN ISTRUMENTO DE DIÓS Y

DE NUETRA VIRGENCITA DE GUADALUPE

MI TESTIMONIO YO SUFRIA MUCHO POR QUÉ TENIA PROLAPSO UTERINO

MI DOCTORA ME AVIA COMENTADO DE UNA POSIBLE CIRUGIA ESTAVA TAN ASUSTADAD POR QUÉ LO QUE NOS QUERIA ERA UNA CIRUGIA PERO UN DÍA ESTUVO DE VISITACION LA SEÑORA VIVIAN CON EL CUADRO DE LA RÉPLICA DE LA VIRGENCITA DE GUADALUPE EN UNA PARROQUIA Y FUI CÓMO UNA HORA IMEDIA DE DISTANSIA Y LA SEÑORA VIVIAN ISO ORACIÓN POR MI CUÁNDO PUSO SU MANO EN EN MI VIENTRE SENTI ALGO MUY CALIENTE Y COMO SI ALGO SE SUBIO Y PARA LA GRORIA DE DIÓS NO NESESITO NIGUNA SIRUGIA ESTOY TOTALMENTE SANA LA DOC-

TORA DISE QUÉ ESTA TODO BIEN NOSAVEN
CÓMO PERO NO NESESITO NIGUGUNA CIRU-
GIA TODO SEA PARABLA GRORIA DE DIÓS Y
POR LA INTERCESIÓN DE NUETRA SEÑORA
DE GUADALUPE

# Testimonio

Del poder de Dios y la intercesión de la Virgencita.

Mi nombre es Olga Herrera, soy de Costa Rica y vivo en New Jersey .

El 17 de Noviembre 2022,  en Costa Rica Dios nos bendijo con un nietito hermoso. El doctor les había dicho a mis hijos que era muy poco probable que ellos pudieran quedar embarazados, pero Dios les dio el milagro de ser los papás de Arturito.

Arturito un niño que en todo el embarazo no hubo ningún problema, fue un embarazo muy deseado y saludable .

Él nació y todo parecía perfecto, pero cuando el pediatra lo examinó le escuchó un soplo en el corazón el cual lo refirió a hacerle un ecocardiograma para descartar cualquier mal. Pero las noticias no fueron nada alentadoras, le diagnosticaron dos cardiopatias que le cobrarían la vida en pocos días. Esos momentos fueron terribles y muy dolorosos .

Lloramos y le suplicabamos a Dios nos ayudará y pidimos a la Virgencita su intersección.

En el consultorio estaba la secretaria y ella sin

saber si eramos creyentes y sin conocernos me entregó en mis manos una medalla bendecida que ella había traído de la misma cátedral en México . Ese momento apesar de mi gran dolor por la noticias me lleno de fe y esperanza, con ese gesto la Virgencita me estaba diciendo que ella estaba con nosotros y protegería a Arturito.

Apartir de ese momento empezó un proceso muy difícil y doloroso. Los médicos hicieron junta médica y les dijeron a los padres de Arturito que ellos no podían hacer nada por el bb , que solo le podían ofrecer cuidados paliativos hasta que el muriera, porqué el daño de él no podían operar en Costa Rica ya queno tenían el equipo para la cirugía. Esa es la peor noticia que unos padres pueden recibir. Pero ahí empezó Dios actuar en corazón de Arturito. Ya que el médico contactó al hospital de Texas Children's Hospital y ahí si podían hacer la cirugía pero el costo era demasiado elevado, los trámites había que hacerlos en corto plazo ya que Arturito solo le daban 6 días de vida. Pero Dios en su misericordia nos puso muchos ángeles en el camino y nos fue abriendo las puertas para toda la documentación y miles de personas unidas en oración y con sus donación Arturito salió rumbo a Houston en un avión Ambulancia el sábado 26 de noviembre y fue operado 6 días después con una cirugía corazón abierto y menos invasiva como los doctores lo creían. El pequeño corazón de Arturito movió miles de corazones en oración. Aún debemos de orar por él y por todos los niños .

La Virgencita siempre nos acompañó, fueron tantas manifestaciones de amor y bondad.

Cada día le agradezco a Dios por el regalo hermoso que es Arturito y seguimos orando para que la Virgencita lo cubra con su manto y la haga un hombre de bien, con un corazón lleno de amor para servir y amar a Dios.

La Virgencita de Guadalupe lo lleva de su mano, él es un niño guerrero y hermoso a quien amamos y glorifico a Dios por el milagro y la Virgencita nunca nos ha dejado solos. La Virgencita de Guadalupe llego a manos de mi hija antes que Arturito naciera. Esa mantita lo acompañó siempre en su camita en el hospital y aún lo acompaña en su camita en Costa Rica.

Dios me los bendiga.

# TESTIMONIO

*Febrero 21, 2023*

Pérdida sentido de sabor y olfato por ls enfermedad de Párkinson ,

Hola ; Mi nombre es Mara. Padesco de la enfermedad de Parkinson. Desde el 2009. Y desde hace 10 años no tenía el sentido de Olfato y gusto. Mi hermana; que es muy Devota me invitó a participar del Rosario del Dia de hoy 20 de febrero. Donde al final oro por todoos@ ; la Sra vivian. Comenze a sentir un olor muy fuerte de Amonia y sentir mi garganta muy seca. Fui y corte un limon y lo olí y probé. Muy Rico. ( por cierto) Gracias Dios por tus Maravillosa experiencia.Gracias Vivian por ser instrumento maravilloso de Dios.Señor en ti Confío. Amen. Amen y Amen.

# Testimonio del hígado

Hace unos días casualmente hablando con la Sra. Vivían le pedí de favor orar por mi hija Paola por que a ella le sale hígado graso ella siempre está en chequeos médicos debido a un tratamiento médico para la piel y el hígado le sale los enzimas altos desde que tenia 13 años ya hoy ella tiene 24 Justo la siguiente semana mi hija tenía exámenes de sangre como siempre parte chequeo rutinario el cual yo no sabia que ya era tiempo de hacérselo mi sorpresa fue que llega a casa y me dise mama me dieron la prescripción para continuar el tratamiento la doctora dise que mi hígado está bien y mi colesterol también.

inmediatamente le dije gracias a Dios y a la Virgencita, la Sra. Vivían está orando por ti. Ella volverá a repetir los exámenes médicos pronto pero se que este resultado será el de siempre en cada test.

Gracias a Dios y a la virgencita y muchas gracias a la Sra. Vivían por orar por mi hija Paola se que es el comienzo de los milagros en ella y la sanacion de su piel

# TESTIMONIO

*Enero 23,2023 Rosario por Zoom*

Créame que desde que e estado en Rosario no había visto la virgen así como la vi aquel día Le vi sus lágrimas en el cuello en la quijada le vi de otro color la piel su ojito lleno de ladrimas hay Dios. Una cosa hermosa quede con la boca callada
  Colombia

# Testimonio

*Rosario por Zoom*

Hola hermanos , quiero compartir mis experiencias con el santo rosario y la imagen de nuestra madre de Guadalupe , sufro de ansiedad tremenda desde hace 25 años con todo y tratamientos no he avanzado mucho, pero para gloria de Dios estos 2'rosarios con el espíritu Santo que nos envía la hermana Vivían , voy sintiendo mucho descanso voy respirando un poco más profundo y las taquicardias duran menos yo la verdad creo que voy a sanar después de 25 años que no veía ya la esperanza, tengo medicamento pero está unción con nuestra madre es directo al corazon, directo al daño emocional por que su mirada tan viva es eficaz y sanadora, creamos oremos con el corazón y tocaremos el cielo.

# TESTIMONIO

*Mexico*

SOY GLORIA Y YANETH DURAN
soy de Colombia chiquinquira
quiero decirles que tengo tres hijos los cuales yo
maltrataba física verbalmente y psicológica mente
tenia un marido que me golpeaba el padre de mis
y hijos también con muchísima groserías lo cual yo
no le veía sentido a nada por tanto maltrato era solo
sufrimiento un día llegó una señora llamada maribel
a golpear dónde yo vivo ella vio en las condiciones
que estaba mi vida lo cual empezó a decir que si
quería entrar a un rosario de la virgen de Guadalupe lo cual yo le dije que de pronto pues yo soy
católica pero no iba a iglesia ni casi oraba hicimos
una oración yo le comente mis problemas y ella vio
como era mi vida como al mes le dije a ella que
como era para yo entrar al rosario lo cual me dijo
que era todos los martes yo entre y no sabia como
se resaba el rosario y con ayuda de toda las del
grupo aprendí comente todo lo que me estaba pa-

sando sentía miedo nervios no casi no les hablaba me daba nervios hablarles poco a poco vivían me fue hablando dándome consejos junto con algunas del grupo y cuando la señora patricia un día le mando a la señora maribel unos pañitos de la virgencita me dieron para cada hijo mío y para mi desde entonces cuando puedo he entrado al rosario le pido con Mucha fe a dios y ala virgen que todo lo que me pasa se pueda curar he tenido cambio en mi vida no es fácil pero tampoco imposible ya no le doy maltrato a mis hijos confío muchísimo en la oración por que cada que hacemos oración es una paz y bien sea a alguno de mis hijos le sale escarcha o a mi mi hijo tiene 9 años y me sufrió una bacteria al cerebro y gracias a dios primeramente y comente el proceso de mi hijo a Vivían y ella con su oración y con el aceite y la fe que uno debe tener en los milagros de mi la vida se que provienen de nuestra madre la virgencita por que desde hace año y medio mi vida a cambiado poco a poco y quiero seguir cambiando por que seque que tengo que luchar por mis dos hijas mi hijo gracias y se si hay fe no habrá nada pero nada iamposible se que la virgencita por muy lejos que este ella nos escucha por que sabe el dolor y la angustia que uno vive gracias por todo madre mía.

# TESTIMONIO

Vivian Mestey aw que linda la Virgencita como manifiesta su amor.

Se recuerda que hace 10 años le lleve a mi bebe para oración por el murmur en el corazón en la cual usted me dijo q no debo de preocuparme que nada mas tengo q tener fe y orar y así fue confié en Dios y en la Virgencita,mi hija todo el tiempo estuvo bien creciendo saludable los chequeos con el cardiólogo ya no eran tan seguido ya que no presentaba síntomas y hoy ya a sus 10 años ya esta de alta con el cardiólogo y el murmur desapareció.

ella duerme con su pañito todas las noches nunca lo deja.

Gloria a Dios y a la Virgencita.

Espero verlas la próxima semana.

# Testimonio

Para gloria del Padre y nuestra madre  de Guadalupe do testimonio que el martes 13 de Junio estábamos reunidas por Zoom haciendo El Rosario a nuestra made y mi cabeza y mi estómago que por varios días me ha estado molestando y sin poder conseguir que el dolor pasara con medicamento. Esa noche Vivían me pidió colocarme en mi cabeza el sagrado manto y comenzó a orar por mi después de unos minutos de oración el dolor desapareció y todas las que estábamos en El Rosario nuestras manos estaban con escarchas y la imagen de nuestra Madre de Guadalupe también se lleno de escarchas Fue una noche maravillosa y bendecida, el dolor ha desaparecido Gracias Madrecita de Guadalupe y gracias Vivían por tus oraciones.

# TESTIMONIO

*Patricia González*

Cuando conocí a Vivian a través de su grupo del Rosario de la Guadalupe, qué es a través de su Ministro de Sanación nos explicar, qué ya siendo parte de grupo la Virgen siempre los tendra con su escarchas por siempre. Yo si le CREI. Pero, creerlo y vivir lo es diferente. Yo estaba mala de mi espalda y mi piernas, cuando fui sanada a través de la Intercesión de Nuestra Virgen Madre y su Humilde Servidora Vivian todo en El Nombre de Nuestro Padre Celestial y nada menos por el ZOOM esa noche. Estuve muchísimas escarchas esa noche...

Después en otro Grupo Sagrado de Rosario estaba mal, la noche antes donde Vivian me habló y me Oro. Pero, yo tenia qué hacer mi trabajo con el otro grupo de Rosario de qué tenía un problema y una preocupación pero me di cuenta qué en el piso tenia escarchas espere el final del Rosario y algo me torció el estómago y hablar ya qué esta otra

persona cuando dice, Mari quiere decir algo, yo
quería esconderme de la pena por qué Ella también La Virgen le dice cositas. Ya qué no me gusta
hablar y escribir. Pero como ELLAS me dicen los
testimonio son para La Gloria de Dios y Su Exci-
tiencia. Por no faltar el respecto de ambos grupos
di mi testimonio de como tenia Las manos llenas
de Escarchas y el piso, ya que estaba angustiada
de qué mi trabajo para este grupo no se me iba
dar. Ahi, me di cuenta lo que Vivian los dices en su
grupo de su Rosario y Sanación por ZOOM. Que
La Virgencita siempre nos tendrá con su Sello, su
«Escarchas». No fue esto solo.. Pues yo estaba
mal otro dia, Vivian me llamo de la nada. Ella me
habló y me dio La Bendición. Al otro dia Voy y me
pongo lapi de labios y tenia una escarcha sobre mi
labio y la deje. Me pongo una máscara y le hablé a
unas cuantas personas donde estuve bajando me
la máscara para qué me entendieran. Pues llegó
a la casa y todavía tenia la escarcha sólo que se
me subió para el lado de la nariz. Me asusté ya
qué no sabía por que yo estava teniendo tantas
escarchas. Pero con gran confianza se la entrege
a La Virgencita ya qué por conocer a Vivian, ahora se lo cierto, la Bendiciónes y sus Oraciones de
Vivian te sella para siempre con la aprobación y el

toque de La Madre Nuestra «Las Escarchas». Es caminar con La Virgencita de una mano y con la otra mano con Vivian. Oremos para qué Vivian y su Familia sean

Bendecida dos y Protejidos

# Testimonio Sagrado Paño

*Monterrey N.L. Mexico*

Mi nombre es Leticia Cazares Flores, vivo en Monterrey, N.L. México, en el año 2020 el mes de Julio ocurrieron en mi vida varios eventos que me llevaron a un estrés y gran preocupación derivado de eso tuve un infarto cerebral el cual duro segundos pero que me ocasionaron consecuencias dolorosas, me sentia muy mal estuve con tratamientos, exámenes, medicamentos y especialistas para sacarme adelante del problema pero yo no lograba sentirme mejor unido a eso tuve ansiedad tambien atendendiendome con psiquiatra y psicólogo estaba muy triste, no dormía, lloraba por las noches pues sentía que moría y al no tener descanso eso me afectaba mucho sentía angustia y perdía con facilidad la tranquilidad aún teniendo todo el amor y apoyo de mi familia.

Un día mi hija menor llegó a verme con una gran noticia, una amiga que acababa de enterarse de lo que me pasó me envió una sabanita con la imagen de la Virgen de Guadalupe para que la tuviera a mi lado y así fue, al recibirla sentí una alegría tan grande, supe en mi corazón que ella venía para ayudarme, para cuidarme recordarme que no estaba sola que me amaba y sabía por lo que estaba pasando, todos los días la tenía en mi pecho, rezaba el rosario con ella, le daba gracias por haber llegado cuando más la necesitaba me sentía más amada que nunca, poco a poco fui recuperándome, por otra parte los médicos no saben a la fecha que fue lo que me provocó el infarto porque gracias a Dios y a la intercesión de nuestra Madre no ha quedado ninguna secuela en mi organismo que por lo general sucede en estos casos y en mi era el cerebro, extremidades y corazón en los que había tenido mayor malestar y que indicaban podrían ser los afectados por el infarto, ellos se sorprendían que no hubiera llegado a más o se hubiera repetido.

Yo, lo único que se, es que fue un milagro de Dios por la intercesión de la Virgen María que con sus palabras llenas de amor «No se turbe tu corazón nos estoy yo aquí que soy tu Madre « me llenaron de consuelo, fortaleza y confianza haciendo crecer más mi fe.

Hoy sigo en tratamiento cada vez con menos medicamentos y con mucha alegría, cuidando más de mi cuerpo y más consciente de como debo llevar mi vida.

Doy mi testimonio con mucho agradecimiento a Dios y a nuestra Madre que desde hace tiempo se hizo presente en mi vida y me ha llevado a conocer a su hijo Jesús quien ha tenido misericordia de mi ya que había muchas cosas que no estaban bien en mi y que yo misma estaba provocando, con esta experiencia se que por algo Dios lo permitio para mí bien ahora trabajo para superarlas e ir corrigiendo con la ayuda de nuestra Madre que de su mano nos lleva para enseñarnos el camino hacia nuestro Señor Jesucristo. Dios les bendiga.

# TESTIMONIO DE INFARTO:

*Febrero 24, 2022*

Muy buenas tarde me llamo Sylvia quiero contarle mi testimonio. Hace dos años comenzen en el grupo de oración de la Sra. Vivian Mestey. Atravez de Zoom cuando comenzo la pandemia del Covic. Mi Fe habia sido probada hace unos años atras cuando sufri de una terrible depresión. Esta pasada semana mi Fe fue puesta a prueba nuevamente. Saben soy una persona diabetica y alta presion el viernes 18 de febrero pase el dia muy bien me dolia un poco el brazo izquierdo yo pense que era de la vacuna del tétano. Cuando llego la noche me dierón unas nauseas y comenze a vomitar pues vomite tanto que inmediatamente mis hijos me llevarón al hospial. Estaba completamente desidratada y me pego a doler el brazo izquierdo y el pecho era un infarto que me estaba dando. Pues me enviarón a un hosital cercano donde tambien tratan personas del corazón. Pues me atendierón y me dejarón hospitalizada y al otro dia me hicerón un cataterismo.

Pero gracias a mi Dios y la Virgencita de Guadalupe salio todo bien. No tengo ninguna alteria tapada ella la Virgencita de Guadalupe estuvo siempre a mi lado. Me enviarón rapido del hospital ya al otro dia de darme de alta ya yo estaba de pie. Muy bien saben ella la Virgen de Guadalupe siempre hace el Milagro y mi Señor y mi Virgencita estuvieron a mi lado. Hoy en dia me preguntan cuando me ven «nena pero a ti no te dio un infarto ? «y yo le digo, si me dio y ya estas caminando ? y yo si gracias a Dios y a la Virgencita mi Bendecido Pañito estuvo todo el tiempo conmigo, me cuido todo el tiempo. Cuando se pide con fe todo se puede y nos escuchan.

# TESTIMONIO DE SANACIÓN:

*8/26/2020*

Conozco a Vivían desde hace más de 40 años ella es mi amiga-hermana y he sido testigo de su crecimiento espiritual y de su maravillosa relación con la Sagrada Virgen y su Hijo. Durante esté tiempo hemos vivido juntas los mejores momentos de nuestras vidas y los mas amargos y tristes también. Hace mas de 1 mes me queje con ella sobre una protuberancia(chichon) que salía en diferentes partes frente por las noches muchas veces acompañado de dolor fuerte de cabeza, después que me levantaba duraba 4 a 5 horas y desaparecía, mi doctora lo estaba tratando con medicamentos para la alérgia que no funcionaban. Vivían decidió orar, ella en West Virginia USA y yo en Puerto Rico, cuando comenzó su oración sentí una muy fuerte presión en la frente acompañada de un soplo como de aire suave y constante que se mantuvo por un gran rato, luego poco dominio de mi cuerpo y después una gran sensación bienestar.

Terminamos agradeciendo a Dios y a su Santa
Madre su ayuda y hasta hoy mes y medio después
no ha pasado más y me siento muy bien
    Vivían te admiro y te amo

# TESTIMONIO

*Niñita de 7 años, Enero 22,2022*

Buenas tardes mi nombre es Sandra Petete y tengo una sobrina de 7 años en Colombia , su nombre Amy Tello q empezó a tener episodios de desmayos en noviembre del 2021 , pérdidas de conocimiento o ligeros temblores, inmediatamente se llevó al urgencias y acá empezó la angustia de toda la familia, todos los exámenes todos con neurólogos pediatra a ver cuál era el problema. Con la triste noticia q le encontraron una masa debajo del cerebelo exactamente el 24 de diciembre de 2021 y necesitaba urgentemente una cirugía. Inmediatamente llamé a Vivían para que me ayudara con su oración a nuestra virgencita de Guadalupe a la que le tengo una fé inmensa por ser tan milagrosa y además la fé y la oración que es tan poderosa siempre hace milagros . Vivían empezó a orar mucho por mi sobrina Amy y en Colombia empezó todo el proceso, desde transportarla a Bogota la Capital , parecía imposible pues era festivo y no había nada disponible , finalmente todo empezó a salir Perfecto , cuando llego al hospital pediátrico en Bogota , efectivamente el médico Pediatra Neurólogo inmediatamente decidió q tenía q hacer cirugía de emergencia , pero con tanta bendición q la masa de 4 cms que sacaron resultó benigna, la cirugía fue un éxito, La Niña en este momento está en recuperación y no va a necesitar ni si quiera quimioterapia. Gracias Vivían, gracias virgencita de Guadalupe por tantos milagros juntos, mi fe cada ve crece más y el poder de la oración son bendiciones multiplicadas . Gracias, Gracias

# TESTIMONIO
# COVID POR ZOOM

*Enero 27, 2022 - Mexico - RC*

Annia empezó con fuertes dolores de cabeza y mucho frío, le dieron medicamento pero no reaccionó, estuvo así durante 3 o 4 días, cambio de médico y mejoró un poco, se hizo la prueba de covid en sangre y salió negativo, después de esos días ya tenía dificultad para respirar, sentía muy oprimido su pecho y bastante agitación, la oxitometria empezó a bajar a 84 y pensábamos que era asma, localizamos a otro médico y le pidió hacerse otra prueba de covid con hisopo y salió positivo a covid, el médico me habló por teléfono y me dijo que su situación era difícil porque se le escuchaban los pulmones saturados y no era asma y urgía que la atendieran y que no perdieramos tiempo. Nos hicieron el favor de localizar a la Neumóloga y le empezaron a poner oxigeno y a inyectar recibiendo todo su tratamiento en casa, eso ayudó a que usted Vivian le hiciera oración frente a la Virgen de Guadalupe, la primer noche puso su foto frente a la Virgen, y el día siguiente fuimos a realizarle estudios de sangre y tomografía para saber si tenía daños en sus pulmones y afortunadamente y gracias a Dios los análisis de sangre salieron bien, la tomografía reveló una neumonía, ese día se agitaba mucho, en la noche hubo veneración a la Santísima Vírgen de Guadalupe y pedí que se le hiciera oración, frote una blusa de mi hija ante la Virgen y se la puso, durmió con la blusa y hoy amaneció muy bien, su rostro alegre, le volvió el color chapeadito, descansó la mayor parte de la noche y la oxitometria subió a 90 para la gloria de Dios y la Santísima Vírgen, está comiendo bien, se bañó y ya habla sin agitarse. Agradezco a nuestra Madre del cielo la sanación que está haciendo en mi hija Annia y a usted Vivian sus oraciones y apoyo en el momento que más lo necesitábamos.

# TESTIMONIO

*5/30/2021*

Buenas noches, hola yo soy Maribel la hermana de Esperanza Hernandez de Colombia;

Le pedimos a Vivian que le rezara a mi hermana que estaba muy grave. Y fue al medico y ellos no podían decir que tenia. Ya no se podía parar, ni moverse y tenia un aogo que le impedía respirar. Pensaban que era un paro renal, algo cardiaco o Lupus.

Entonces Vivian me dijo «ponle agua bendita y aceite bendito y ponerle el Sagrado Paño sobre su pecho. Mi hermana cerro los ojos y se fue en descanso o se durmió. Cuando se desperto Vivian le pregunto "Como te siente, y me hermana le dijo «siento movimientos en las manos. Y mi herma-na comenzó a decir lo que sintio cuando estaba en descanso. Dijo que "sintió como si le hubiesan puesto una injección en la vena, como un suero por vena y caliente". Ella siguió diciendo "que se sentía mejor y que el calor era por todo su cuerpo".

Vivian volvió a rezarle y le dijo "ponga sus manos en la rodilla". Otra vez me hermana decía que se sentía mejor. Entonces Vivian le dijo" se puede sentar ? y mi hermana se sento. Que ella no podía hacer eso por si sola. Vivian volvió a rezarle. Mi hermana seguía diciendo que se sentía mejor y que el calor estaba en todo su cuerpo. ¿Entonces Vivian le dijo' Se puede parar? Mi hermana le dijo si me puedo parar. Yo casi ni puedo respirar cuando la vi parase. Dios mio que emoción demasiado de impresionante, nunca había vivido un Milagro así, tan claro al frente de mis ojos. Fue una bendición ver como

la cara de mi hermana cambio. Ya se parecía a ella. Cuando comenzamos mi hermana se veía moribunda. Yo me siento que no soy la misma que he cambiado. Entonces le dije vamos a caminar y camino por toda la casa. Mi esposo estaba ahí y no lo podía creer. Luego ella siguió hablando y como si nada. Gracias Dios por este Milagros la Gloria es tuya. Gracias Virgen de la Guadalupe por interceder. Y gracias Vivian por ser obediente al llamado de la Virgen y Jesus.

# TESTIMONIO

*11/13/2020*

Mi nombre es Patricia

cuando me uní hacer El Rosario con la Sra. Vivían Mastey a nuestra Madrecita la Virgen de Guadalupe, tenía varios meses que venía sintiendo que cuando hablaba me faltaba el aire.

No podía tener una conversación sin tomar una pausa de segundos para continuar.

En uno de los rosarios quise hacer un misterio pero me tocó pedir que me ayudaran pues no podía hacerlo sola. Vivían me pidió que colocara el sagrado manto de nuestra madrecita de Guadalupe en mi garganta y hacía lo hacía en los rosarios siguientes!

Lo más hermoso es que este síntoma ya no está con migo para la gloria de Dios y nuestra Madre.

Nunca,nose porque di las gracias a nuestra madre la Virgencita,nose porque?

Pero en El Rosario de anoche Noviembre 12 al terminar El Rosario como siempre lo hacemos,

Vivían invoca al Espíritu Santo imponiendo sus manos sobre cada uno de los participantes, sentí la Gracias del llanto y me mostraba que ya no me faltaba el aire para la gloria de Dios Padre!el escucha nuestras súplicas atraves de nuestra Madre Maria!

Amen!!

# TESTIMONIO

*10/28/2020*

Mi nombre es Patricia González y quiero dar mi testimonio hoy Octubre 27 después de terminar El Rosario a nuestra Virgencita de Guadalupe con la Señora Vivian Mestey en el grupo de oración el cual ella dirige los Martes y Jueves nuestra Madrecita se manifestó dejándome sus escarchas en mis manos para Gloria de Jesús su hijo!

una vez más tu misericordia me ha visitado señor Amen! Amen!

# TESTIMONIO

*Monterray, Mexico - Monica Sanchez*

Yo trabajo en una Heladería y utilizamos nieves y cargamos los botes grandes y duele la mano y el brazo Y yo tenía mucho dolor lo único que pensé aún no tengo el paño pero está la imagen en su página se me ocurrió poner la imagen de la Virgen de Guadalupe la del paño en mi brazo y con mucha fe, le pedí que intercediera por el dolor que sentía, era un dolor como si se me desgarrada el músculo de mi brazo y después de pedirle a la Virgen que intercediera ante su hijo Jesús que me quitará el dolor en de, se me quitó Es fecha que ya no me ha dolido. Ya no me volvió el dolor la Virgen intercedió, gracias Sra. Vivian por compartir a nuestra Madre, gracias a la página por difundir la devoción de nuestra Madre Virgen de Guadalupe.

# Testimonio

*De Monterry - Mexico 10/9/2020*

Conocí a Vivian hace más de 4 años en la iglesia de St Reymond cuando trajo la Virgen. Vivian me regalo un Manto y en aquel momento le pedí que orara por mis hijos. Desde entonces he tenido muy poco contacto con ella.

Limpiando mi cuarto encontré una estampa de la Virgen de Guadalupe, cuando la vi quien vino a mi mente fue Vivian. Le mande un mensaje y le pedí por favor que orara por alguien muy querido, Julio. Le expliqué brevemente lo que estaba pasando. Julio fue diagnosticado con Covid en junio. Le conté que estaba en el hospital desde 30 de junio, pero el 2 de agosto había sido trasladado a ICU. Acudí a Vivi desesperada por que Julio estaba conectado a un ventilador y muy grave.

Yo estaba en constante oración pero sentía que a pesar de que habían mucha gente rezando no era suficiente y Viví me podía ayudar.

Vivian me hablo del grupo para que me uniera a rezar el Rosario con ellos. Realmente no lo hice. Pero cuando Julio iba a ser desconectado del ventilador sentí la necesidad de unirme a ellos para rezar. Nunca se me olvidare, traté y no podía entrenar. Lo logre tarde y me uní a ellos en oración. El 16 de septiembre Julio fue desconectado del ventilador. Esa noche Vivian rezo fuertemente por el y por mi familia.

Desde entonces comenzó mi fuerte unión a la Virgen, cada día que pasa siento más la necesidad de la oración y mi alabanza a Dios.

La entrega en oración y mi cercanía a Dios y la Virgen me ha llevado a tener fuertes manifestaciones. El domingo 4 de octubre encontré en mi carro al lado del freno algo impresionante, una pluma blanca. El lunes le mande la foto a Viví, sostuve la pluma en mis mano algo maravilloso. Pero cuando estaba mirando la me di cuenta que tenía Escarcha en mis manos.

En ese momento sentí tanto gozo, lloré pero de alegría. No sabía lo que me estaba pasando. Viví me llamo y me dijo la Virgencita se está manifestando en ti.

El martes fue con el sacerdote y le enseñé mis manos estaban llenas de Escarcha el se dio cuenta. Me pregunto que si estaba orando mucho. Le conté todo lo que estaba pasando. Me dijo es un Bendición muy grande tienes que escuchar el llamado. Desde entonces siento que mi vida a cambiado. Siento Paz y Gozo.

No piensen que no hay problemas Julio a seguido con sus alta y bajas pero yo confío en Papá Dios y mi querida Madre. Ellos tiene el control.

Abre tu corazón a Dios y ora es el arma más poderosa. Believe!!! Los Milagros existen.....Dios y la Virgen los protejan.

Vivian gracias por tu bella amistad y tu entrega... Bendiciones TQM Glory

# Testimonio

*August 16, 2020*

Buenas tardes, señora Vivian Mestey quiero compartir contigo desde que estoy en el grupo de oración he visto que mi vida ha cambiado. Yo conocía de Dios por mi mama. Pero solo era ir a misa los domingos, pero no me dedicaba a orar como lo hago ahora. Si señora yo nunca había estado en esa relación, por eso doy gracias a Dios por ir poco a poco seguir su camino. Y que el haga de mí su voluntad. Ahora confió más en Dios, estoy mas en tranquila en paz mis problemas en mi hogar han mejorado. Porque estaba a punto de divorciarme, pero Dios y la Virgensita me han dado la fortaleza para seguir luchando. Y seguiré orando con fe para ver mas cambios en mi vida.

# Testimonio De Fe

*FZ*

Muchas gracias, nunca se me olvida la vez q la conocí q yo lloraba desconsoladamente y usted me dijo pero donde esta tu Fe esas palabras me han ayudado mucho y de ahí en adelante he aprendido a confiar en Dios y entregarme por completo a su voluntad y humillarme ante El, tener un corazón lleno de su Paz y amor he tenido muchas vivencias hermosas y de verdad he sentido su presencia en mi corazón. Y en todo mi proceso de enfermedad no se como expresar cada manifestación en mi vida.

# TESTIMONIO

*April 30th, 2020*

Grupo de Oracion, Quiero darles un testimonio de sanacion. Que nuestra señora madre de Guadalupe me ah regalado este primer día del santo rosario de el martes pues en el santo rosario yo sentí mucho calor demasiado fuerte del cual hasta mis poros de mi cabeza sentía y la espalda un calor que me quemaba y que al terminar el santo rosario nuestra hermana vivían pregunto a cada una de nuestras hermanas que nos unimos en oración. Cual fe nuestro testimonio que la madre nos hizo sentir y ya comentando mi sentir era un gozo una alegría lo que mi corazón sentía y nuestra hermana Vivían nos comentó que Atravez de los días la madre se manifestaría y haci fue para la gloria de Dios vivián me pregunto que si yo en ese momento pasaba por alguna situación de alguna enfermedad y me dijo bueno si no quieres decir no te preocupes y la verdad si estaba pasando por unos días que me preocupaba por que yo había estado con una bacteria en vías urinarias de cual yo ya había tenido varios tratamientos que mi urólogo me había dado pero dejaba de tomar antibióticos y volvía y exactamente tenía como dos semanas que estaba orinándo muy fuerte que me preocupe otra vez aún tomando mucha agua y este y el miércoles que me levante y fui al baño me di cuenta que el el olor fétido y color amarillo se fue sentí en mi corazón lo que vivían nuestra hermana me había dicho que la madre se manifestaría me sano de ese olor fétido que sentir miedo pensé ahora con esta pandemia como iré al médico pero para la Gloria de Dios y madre María santicima estoy Sanada.

# TESTIMONY

---

*Depresión Severa, Enero 2018*

Mi nombre es Slyvia Diaz de Puerto Rico. Le voy a contar de mi testimonio, yo tenia un dolor de cabeza fuerte y no se me quitaba. Me hicierón cuantos estudios excitia y no me encontraban nada.

Un dia la Sra. Vivian me llama para hablar conmigo y preguntarme como estaba? Yo le conte y ella me invito a Connericut a la iglesia que ella iba a estar. Ando a la Virgen de Guadalupe y ella oro por mi y me dijo «No tienes nada, estas Sanada».

Y estuve en la misa y despues pase lor la Imagen de Guadalupe y la toque. Y sali de la iglesia , yo casi no podia caminar y casi no podia hablar. Estaba pasando por una depresión, pasaron unos dias y segui mejorando y poco a poco saegui saliendo de la depresión. El dolor de cabeza mejoro porque el medicamento no me hacia nada. Gracias que fui y toque a la Imagen de la Virgen. Fue un Milagro que pude salir de esa depressión. Gracias a la Virgen de Guadalupe. A esas personas que No creen deverian creer porque mi Virgencita de Guadalupe hizo el Milagro y me saco del infierno que estaba viviendo, y ahora mismo estoy muy bien y muy feliz.

# Testimonio

Me habían diagnosticado have 9 años con diverticula y este día 18 de Agosto 2023, la sangre preciosa de Jesucristo me lavo mis intestinos! No encontraron rastro de eso, ademas mi doctor no me había dicho pero había sospecha de un tumor maligno y para la Gloria de Dios y la intercesión de la virgen santísima amantisima mi madrecita bella no hay nada! Gloria a ti Señor Jesús! Bendito seas! Alabado sea tu Santo y Glorioso nombre! Quien como Dios? Nadie como Dios!

Le pedí a mi virgencita y dormí con mi pañito en el vientre anoche

# Testimonio del Sagrado Paño

Buenas tardes Bibi mira quería compartir que el testimonio de mi hermana María del Rayo donde ella fue auxiliada por el paño de la santísima virgen de Guadalupe hace 15 días más o menos o 20 que estuvo en cama por dengue se sentía tan mal tan mal que ni siquiera podía alcanzar el vaso de agua que tenía al lado ni ni su teléfono no quería moverse con mucha dificultad se conectó al Santo Rosario pero dice que se puso el paño se lo puso y estuvo en el Santo Rosario completo cuando tú pediste el espíritu santo y todo esto ella se quedó dormida cuando vino a despertar pudo levantarse a tomar el agua el medicamento y demás después se volvió a quedar dormida pues ya era la noche pero al amanecer se levantó totalmente renovada que hasta le dijo a mi mamá no quiere que vaya al mercado por algunas cosas para almorzar y le dice a mi mamá pero cómo si tú estás enferma no yo ya me siento muy bien mucho mejor o sea mejoró increíblemente hasta pudo viajar a México al otro día para participar con nuestra señora Rosa mística Gloria a Dios Gloria a María

# Testimonio Sagrado Paño

*Mexico*

Hola buenas noches una disculpa x noamdar mi testimonio vivís estado con la agenda apretada bueno como te comentaba cuando yo abro el paquete saco el pañito de la virgen y Melo pogo en el pecho siento mucha emoción porque yo decía madre hasta que llegaste esperé mucho este momento enpece a llorar mucho yo sentía. Que ella está presente en ese momento tenía los deseos de gritar y decirle lo que yo sentía que como mi madre ya no podía esconder mi dolor fue algo de maciado fuerte empecé a vomitar sabía que en eseemto estaba liberando porque no a mi me apasado en retiros espirituales ante el santísimo pero el dolor que yo sentía por muchas cosas y muy delicadas y que siempre calle por años estoy diciendo esto llorado porque me acuerdo que se me salía de control era demasiado fuerte como si ella estaba viendo de frente de mi ya no pude más me acuerdo que es gritaba muy fuerte que me lleve un trapo a la boca xque no quería que que mi mamá escuchará y no se fuera de a espantar cuando de momento me desmalle ya no supe de. Mi no me pude. Mover por un rato me costo. Mucho pararme. K le ablo no a mi hermana x teléfono que le digo de que es la virgen estaba dasiado fuerte no podía ni ablar k me ayudara xque. Me sentia.muy mal me hizo oración me fui calmando me sentí mejor pero cuando me paro del sillón ya no soy la. Misma algo pasa dentro de mi como una fuerte que no tenía dentro de mi me sentí mucho mejor algo abia hecho la virgen en.mi cuando uno tiene fe la virgen se manifiesta en eso. Pañitos se los puse a unas amigas por qué murió su. Mami y me. Comentaron que. Sintieron. Mucho. Consuelo tanto que al otro día se pusieron unos pañitos que ellas buscaron en casa en una ocasión me puse el pañito de la. Virgen y en el rosario del. Lunes con vivís porque en ese momento yo tenía dengue está muy mal no podía moverme ni pararme muchos deseos de volver el estómago apenas pude prender el cirio y tomar el rosario cuando me pogo el pañito en el sengo misterio me siento mejor recuerdo k. Me dormí cuando yo desperté. Estaban terminando. El rosario estaban dando testimonios me paro de la. Cama. Cómo sin nada cuando yo le comento a.mi. mamá no. Me. Lo creía tanto k le. Comento me voy. A México a visitar a. Mi hermana a ver a la virgen de rosa. Mística x su día ya que. Año con años voy. Así fiesta y a visitar a la villa virgen de Guadalupe pues este es.mi. Testimonio bendiciones gracias. Disculpa por mis letras. Vivís y muchas gracias.

# TESTIMONIO

Buenos días Sra Vivían, el día lunes 31 de julio al irme a dormir me empezó a dar un dolor cabeza con un ardor en la frente y en mis ojos, estuve así hasta el miércoles se agudizaron los dolores, los medicamentos no me sirvieron de nada, me decidí hablarle a la Sra Vivían del ministerio escarchas de l virgen contándole lo que me pasaba, ella empezó a orar por mi y cuando llamo al espíritu Santo, empecé a sentir un calor en la cabeza y empecé a sudar, me quede dormida y hoy por la mañana me pare de la cama a hacer mi almuerzo y note que el dolor habia desaparecido para la gloria de Dios y de la virgen Santísima de Guadalupe

# Testimonio

*Prolapso Uterino*

LE DOY GRACIAS A DIÓS Y A LA SEÑORA VI-
VIAN POR SIEMPRE SER UN ISTRUMENTO DE
DIÓS Y

DE NUETRA VIRGENCITA DE GUADALUPE

MI TESTIMONIO YO SUFRIA MUCHO POR
QUÉ TENIA PROLAPSO UTERINO

MI DOCTORA ME AVIA COMENTADO DE UNA
POSIBLE CIRUGIA ESTAVA TAN ASUSTADAD
POR QUÉ LO QUE NOS QUERIA ERA UNA
CIRUGIA PERO UN DÍA ESTUVO DE VISITA-
CION LA SEÑORA VIVIAN CON EL CUADRO DE
LA RÉPLICA DE LA VIRGENCITA DE GUADA-
LUPE EN UNA PARROQUIA Y FUI CÓMO UNA
HORA IMEDIA DE DISTANSIA Y LA SEÑORA VI-
VIAN ISO ORACIÓN POR MI CUÁNDO PUSO SU
MANO EN EN MI VIENTRE SENTI ALGO MUY
CALIENTE Y COMO SI ALGO SE SUBIO Y PARA
LA GRORIA DE DIÓS NO NESESITO NIGUNA
SIRUGIA ESTOY TOTALMENTE SANA LA DOC-

TORA DISE QUÉ ESTA TODO BIEN NOSAVEN
CÓMO PERO NO NESESITO NIGUGUNA CIRU-
GIA TODO SEA PARABLA GRORIA DE DIÓS Y
POR LA INTERCESIÓN DE NUETRA SEÑORA
DE GUADALUPE

# Testimonio

Buenas tardes bendiciones, sufro desde hace mas de 15 años de colon irritable, gastritis y reflujo gastríco, el reflujo me ha afectado la parte respiratoria me ha dado sinusitis, rinitis, laringitis. Hace 3 semanas como tenía una laringitis me coloqué una inyeccion para desinflamar la garganta pero por error me la colocaron de más miligramos que lo acostumbrado, y eso me ha generado una crisis terrible en mi estomago, ardor, colon inflamado y reflujo , es decir todos los síntomas al mismo tiempo, he tenido noches sin dormir, he visitado como a 4 médicos y no he podido salir de la crisis. Hace como 1 mes por medio de una prima conocí el ministerio de Vivian y he asistido como a 3 rosarios y me acordé de ella en mi angustia y le escribí hace unos días para que orara, y por voluntad de Dios hoy a las 5:30 am después de justamente hacerle el rosario a la Virgencita, me escribió Vivan para decirme que si estaba despierta para que hiciéramos oración, desde allí sentí que la Virgen estaba intercediendo.

Después de la oración se me llenaron las manos de escarchas pequeñitas y de aceite, especialmente la mano que me coloqué para orar por la sanidad de mi estomago tenía 2 escarchas grandecitas, también todo mi estomago estaba lleno de escarchas pequeñitas, Gloria a Dios, nuestro señor Jesús está haciendo una obra de sanidad por la interseción de la Virgen de Guadalupe. Hermanita Dios la bendiga grandemente junto a su familia y bendiga su hermoso ministerio.

# TESTIMONIO DEL SAGRADO PAÑO

Quiero darles las gracias a Nuestra Madrecita Santa desde el Sabado pasado tuve hasta ayer una MIGRAÑA INTENSISIMA, q me tenía muy mal, sin poder dormir ni nada muy decaida, anoche coji el paño de Nuestra Madre de Guadalupe y me lo enrolle en la cabeza antes de dormir y le pedi a la Madre que me ayudara que ya no daba mas... hoy amaneci perfectamente bien...para la Gloria de Dios y honra de nuestra Santisima y purisima Madre Sana Maria de Guadalupe.

# TESTIMONIO

Quiero compartir para gloria de Dios.

Un regalo de nuestra madre de Guadalupe, hace algunos días vengo presentando un dolor de cabeza insoportable pero hoy aumento más me atravesaba las sientes y el centro de la frente ya había tomado una pastilla para éste problema y persistía, pero la hermana Vivian me comparte una foto de nuestra señora de Guadalupe destinada para asistir a los enfermos y yo por impulso acerco la foto desde el celular a mi frente y o bendición el dolor se desvanece como si uno recorriera el dedo sobre la pantalla y cambiará de página el dolor se fue en ese instante me impresione y le narre lo sucedido a Vivian, yo de verdad le dije no conozco está forma tan fuerte de recibir la ayuda celestial no hay explicación sólo algo divino puede obrar asi.

Gracias señor por darnos a vuestra madre de Guadalupe y por derramar tus dones para el bien de la humanidad.

Gracias Vivian por tu apoyo y tu servicio bendiciones para todos.

# Testimonio

Hola, soy Gissell Cuevas Sayas de Colombia. Desde que empecé con el grupo Escarchas of Guadalupe - Vivian Mestey Healing Ministry, me ha llenado de gracias y muchas bendiciones debido a la intercesión de nuestra madre celestial y la misericordia de su hijo Jesús.

1.La primera semana la vi llorando y viendo como cerraba su ojo.

2.Después sentí el corazón de Jesús en su vientre es decir sus latidos fue la segunda gracia que me regalo.

3. Finalmente, la virgen me miro y me regalo las escarchas en la mano y ahora de manera permanente.

4. Por gracia de Dios he recibido el bautismo en el espíritu santo que es el don de lenguas y su interpretación.

5.Recordemos que todo es para glorificar el reino del señor

# TESTIMONIO

pérdida sentido de sabor y olfato por ls enfermedad de Párkinson ,

Hola ; Mi nombre es Mara. Padesco de la enfermedad de Parkinson. Desde el 2009. Y desde
hace 10 años no tenía el sentido de Olfato y gusto.
Mi hermana; que es muy Devota me invitó a participar del Rosario del Dia de hoy 20 de febrero.
Donde al final oro por todoos@; la Sra vivian. Comenze a sentir un olor muy fuerte de Amonia y
sentir mi garganta muy seca. Fui y corte un limon y
lo olí y probé. Muy Rico. ( por cierto) Gracias Dios
por tus Maravillosa experiencia.Gracias Vivian por
ser instrumento maravilloso de Dios.Señor en ti
Confío. Amen. Amen y Amen.

# Testimonio

Buenas tardes bendiciones, sufro desde hace mas de 15 años de colon irritable, gastritis y reflujo gastríco, el reflujo me ha afectado la parte respiratoria me ha dado sinusitis, rinitis, laringitis. Hace 3 semanas como tenía una laringitis me coloqué una inyeccion para desinflamar la garganta pero por error me la colocaron de más miligramos que lo acostumbrado, y eso me ha generado una crisis terrible en mi estomago, ardor, colon inflamado y reflujo , es decir todos los síntomas al mismo tiempo, he tenido noches sin dormir, he visitado como a 4 médicos y no he podido salir de la crisis. Hace como 1 mes por medio de una prima conocí el ministerio de Vivian y he asistido como a 3 rosarios y me acordé de ella en mi angustia y le escribí hace unos días para que orara, y por voluntad de Dios hoy a las 5:30 am después de justamente hacerle el rosario a la Virgencita, me escribió Vivan para decirme que si estaba despierta para que hiciéramos oración, desde allí sentí que la Virgen estaba intercediendo.

Después de la oración se me llenaron las manos de escarchas pequeñitas y de aceite, especialmente la mano que me coloqué para orar por la sanidad de mi estomago tenía 2 escarchas grandecitas, también todo mi estomago estaba lleno de escarchas pequeñitas, Gloria a Dios, nuestro señor Jesús está haciendo una obra de sanidad por la interseción de la Virgen de Guadalupe. Hermanita Dios la bendiga grandemente junto a su familia y bendiga su hermoso ministerio

# TESTIMONY

*Devotion to Our Lady of Guadalupe - December 8*

Candles ( Velitas Colombian tradition)

Las niñas comparten todo el tiempo acá en casa con la abuelita pues ella les dedica mucho tiempo, han visto como mi madre mantiene el paño la mayor parte del tiempo sobre ella en el hombro, y como duermen con ella la han visto aún en las noches dormir con su paño Sagrado sobre ella, así tal cual han visto ellas tratan siempre de hacer lo mismo, cuando las vemos tienen su paño en el hombro, o se lo colocan en el cuello, le dan besos como dicen ellas a la mamá de Jesús, todas desde María De los Angeles que acaba de cumplir 6 años, Sara Isabel de 3, y Luisa Fernanda de 1 año, lo cuidan como pueden, pero lo mantienen cerca de ellas o sobre ellas, pues también duermen con el palo sagrado sobre ellas

También ven a mi madre al despertar hacer el rosario, gracias a Dios tienen esa Gracia

# TESTIMONIO

Mi nombre es Patricia

cuando me uní hacer El Rosario con la Sra. Vivían Mastey a nuestra Madrecita la Virgen de Guadalupe, tenía varios meses que venía sintiendo que cuando hablaba me faltaba el aire.

No podía tener una conversación sin tomar una pausa de segundos para continuar.

En uno de los rosarios quise hacer un misterio pero me tocó pedir que me ayudaran pues no podía hacerlo sola. Vivían me pidió que colocara el sagrado manto de nuestra madrecita de Guadalupe en mi garganta y hacía lo hacía en los rosarios siguientes!

Lo más hermoso es que este síntoma ya no está con migo para la gloria de Dios y nuestra Madre.

Nunca,nose porque di las gracias a nuestra madre la Virgencita,nose porque?

Pero en El Rosario de anoche Noviembre 12 al terminar El Rosario como siempre lo hacemos, Vivían invoca al Espíritu Santo imponiendo sus manos sobre cada uno de los participantes, sentí la Gracias del llanto y me mostraba que ya no me

faltaba el aire para la gloria de Dios Padre!el escucha nuestras súplicas atraves de nuestra Madre
Maria!

Amen!!

# TESTIMONIO

Mi nombre es Patricia González y quiero dar mi testimonio hoy Octubre 27 después de terminar El Rosario a nuestra Virgencita de Guadalupe con la Señora Vivian Mestey en el grupo de oración el cual ella dirige los Martes y Jueves nuestra Madrecita se manifestó dejándome sus escarchas en mis manos para Gloria de Jesús su hijo!

una vez más tu misericordia me ha visitado señor Amen! Amen!

# Testimonio

Buenas tardes, señora Vivian Mestey quiero compartir contigo desde que estoy en el grupo de oración he visto que mi vida ha cambiado. Yo conocía de Dios por mi mama. Pero solo era ir a misa los domingos, pero no me dedicaba a orar como lo hago ahora. Si señora yo nunca había estado en esa relación, por eso doy gracias a Dios por ir poco a poco seguir su camino. Y que el haga de mí su voluntad. Ahora confió más en Dios, estoy mas en tranquila en paz mis problemas en mi hogar han mejorado. Porque estaba a punto de divorciarme, pero Dios y la Virgensita me han dado la fortaleza para seguir luchando. Y seguiré orando con fe para ver mas cambios en mi vida.

# TESTIMONIO

Buenas tardes, señora Vivian Mestey quiero compartir contigo desde que estoy en el grupo de oración he visto que mi vida ha cambiado. Yo conocía de Dios por mi mama. Pero solo era ir a misa los domingos, pero no me dedicaba a orar como lo hago ahora. Si señora yo nunca había estado en esa relación, por eso doy gracias a Dios por ir poco a poco seguir su camino. Y que el haga de mí su voluntad. Ahora confió más en Dios, estoy mas en tranquila en paz mis problemas en mi hogar han mejorado. Porque estaba a punto de divorciarme, pero Dios y la Virgensita me han dado la fortaleza para seguir luchando. Y seguiré orando con fe para ver mas cambios en mi vida.

# Testimonio

Yo asistir al rosario de Vivian Mestey por zoom. Por cuál yo y ella no nos conocíamos anteriormente. Yo estaba preocupada ya qué mi espalda y píes mi dolores son fuerte. Al final de rosario, ella me dijo como estaba de mi piernas y pies, cuando ella no sabia nada de mi.. Mi espalda y mi píes ya no me duelen y ahora estoy llena de escarchas... Bendiciones

# TESTIMONIO

*Diagnostico de Covic y embarazada*

Embarazada tres meses en coma. Ina prima la fue a visitor y llevo el Sagrad Paño. Se lo puso a la barrier de la madre. El bebe comenzo a moverse y a tirar pataditas. A los dos dias a la mama le dierón dos ataques del corazón. Los medicos estaban bregando con la situación y antes del tercer ataque de corazón nacio la bebe por su cuenta. Los medicos no se percatarón que la pequeñita de 1libra y 7onzas habia nacido. Esta experiencia le ha cambiado su vida.

Ambas ya estan en su hogar, la bebe esta en terapias. Una experiencia, vivida bendecida por la Santa Madre y la Gloria de Dios.

# Testimonio

Mi nombre es Milton Guzman vivo en Dover Plains NY originario de Guatemala casado con 4 hijas católico converso del protestantismo desde el 2015. El ano pasado julio 7 2023 tuvimos nuestra cuarta niña como todas han sido por cesárea fuimos hablar con el obispo para que nos diera un permiso para poderse operar a lo cual el obispo dijo que la posición De la Iglesia es estar abierto a la vida. Entonces vamos a planificar del método natural y a mediados de séptiembre mi esposa me dijo que la regla no le venia y le dije que simopre a sido así después de dar a luz, se hizo una prueba y salió positiva, y dije otra niña! No es que las niñas sean malas amo a mis hijas pero siempre quise tener un hijo baron.

Tube el honor de ir a the National Shrine of the Divine Mercy en Massachusetts el dia 11 de diciembre a ver la imagen bendita de nuestra señora de Guadalupe. Frente a su imagen hice pedido que el bebe que esperamos con mi esposa fuera baron, ya tengo 5 niñas y lo mas seguro era que fuera nena, paran mi sorpresa cuando hicieron el gender reveal y mi esposa me llamo porque estaba trabajando y le dije ya se es nena!! Y ella me dijo nooo!!! Es baron y me acorde cuando le pedi a nuestra bendita madre para que intercediera para que fuera baron.

# Testimonio

Hace varios meses me dio un ataque del corazón, y mi recuperación fue Mlagrosa. Por los ultimos dos dias la Virgen de Guadalupe me ha dado la manifestación de Aciete y Escarchas. Estaba en mi cocina, cuando mi mano Izquierda se me lleno de aciete y Escarchas. Y hoy estaba en mi carro, cuando me dio el sol y de nuevo la manifestación del aceite y las Escarchas.

Desde que conoci a Vivian Mestey hace años y tambien asisto al rosario por Zoom, mi vids sigue cambiando. Con tantas bendiciónes y sorry go viviendo el Camino en mi vida, atravez de la Virgen de Guadalupe.

Amen

*www.vivianmestey.com*